HIKARU NOGUCHI

DARNING SOCKS

Why do socks wear out?

Any clothes can become damaged. Socks, in particular, wear out quickly and are often regarded as disposable. First, let's learn how socks wear out.

Friction leads to thinning of the yarn

FRICTION ARISES FROM WEARING OR WASHING → YARN FIBRES WEAR OUT IN AREAS OF HEAVY USE → THE YARN BECOMES WORN, AND THE FABRIC BECOMES TRANSPARENT AND THIN

Socks are often made from natural fibres knitted together with a synthetic fibre, such as nylon. It is used to improve elasticity or the fit, but it's also strong. It is often the case that this thread remains intact even after natural fibres have worn away.

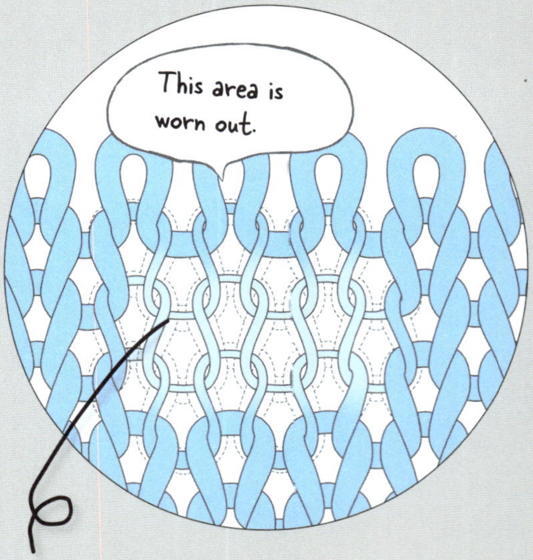

Socks wear out in stages

Thin

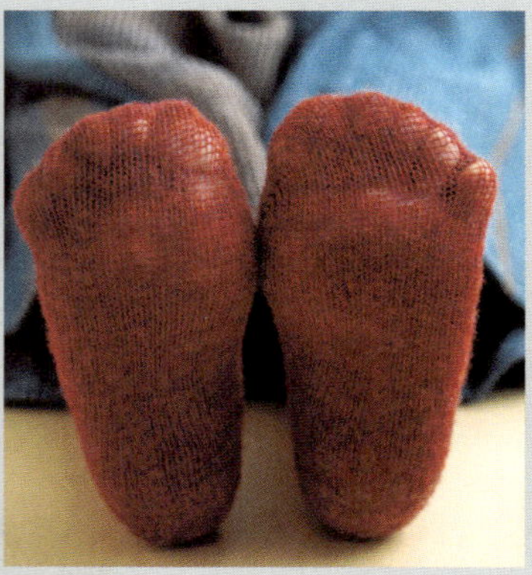

Early darning works best

In this image, the yarn is slightly thinned. If you apply darning at this stage, your socks will last longer.

Thinner

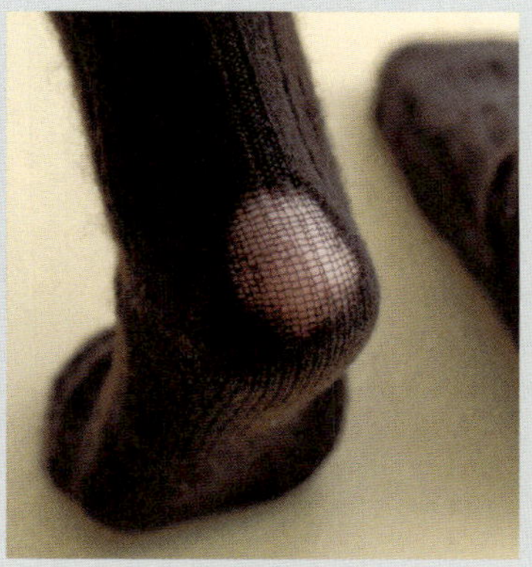

Apply darning now!

At this point the natural yarn is worn out and only the synthetic thread is left. Darning is easier before a hole emerges.

A Hole!

Let's use some tights fabric

Eventually the worn-out area develops into a hole… If you use a patch from some old tights, even if there is a large hole, it will be relatively easy to darn.

If you notice damage to your sock...

When your sock is damaged, you might not know what to do, or you might feel hesitant about repairing it, but it's best to get started right away.

I don't know how to fix it so should I leave it alone?

START DARNING STRAIGHT AWAY.

If you leave your damaged sock, the yarn will wear out further, the top will lose elasticity, and the sock will get worse. It is better to darn before it's too late!

Will darning make the sock uncomfortable to wear?

IT'LL BE FINE!

People worry that the sole of their foot will feel uncomfortable on an uneven surface. Most people are not so sensitive on their feet and unlikely to notice the difference. Even if you do, you will get used to it very quickly.

Even if I repair it, won't it wear out again soon?

Socks are subject to strong friction and will go through continuous damage. But you can make them more durable by choosing the right thread (see page 12). Of course, this doesn't mean it will last forever. Darned areas will still be subject to friction and will likely be damaged again. If you stitch densely for durability, the area could end up being hard and uncomfortable to wear, or make the surrounding area wear out more quickly. The best solution is to darn again when, or if, it gets damaged again (see page 68). Just relax and enjoy darning and nurturing your sock.

DON'T OVERTHINK IT, JUST START DARNING!

Contents

Let's try darning a sock

Darn with me by following the steps on this page.
Once you've had a go, you'll see how fun it is.

Small hole near the toe

The heel is wearing thin too

1 Let's prepare

Tidy up by trimming off the pilling.

Worn-out socks may have pilling or lumps of fluff. If you take away too much, this can damage the sock, so just remove the ones that stand out.

If you turn the sock wrong side (WS) out, there will be fluffy balls. Remove them by hand.

2 Let's choose the thread

Now choose the thread for darning. Referring to pages 12–13, select your preferred thread type. Choose one or several of the colours of the sock and it will blend in. In this case, red and mustard yellow have been chosen.

3

Set the sock on a darning mushroom

Place the sock on a darning mushroom. You can stitch from the front or back. Here, we will stitch from the back, so turn the sock wrong side (WS) out before you put it on the mushroom.

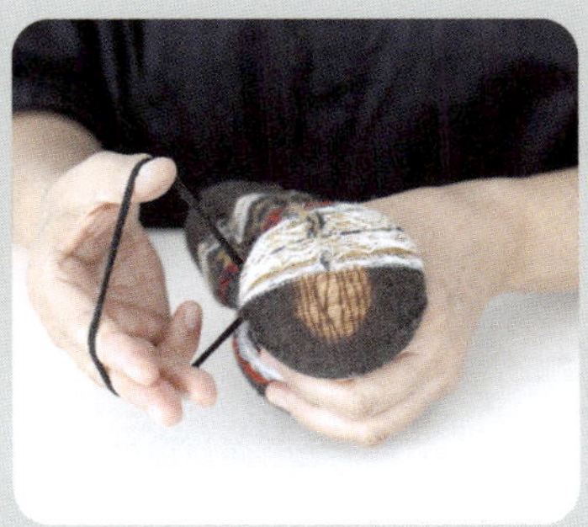

Position the damaged section at the centre of the darning mushroom and hold it in position with a rubber band. Make sure the sock is not too stretched or pulled out of shape.

Mark the area to be darned using chalk 1–2cm ($^{3}/_{8}$in–$^{3}/_{4}$in) outside the damaged area and tack (baste) all around (so you can see it on the other side).

4

Place the tights material on top

Cut out a 20cm (7½in) square of tights material.

Put the tights material on top of the sock and secure it firmly with a rubber band or elastic.

5

Start stitching

Work with an arm's length of yarn – measuring from hand to heart!

Cut an arm's length – about 50cm (20in) – of red yarn.

Work parallel honeycomb stitch (see page 18) using the tacking stitches, visible through the tights material, as a guide.

When the yarn is finished, you can change colour. Here, we change to mustard-yellow and continue stitching.

Finished stitching. Don't worry if the stitches are not tidy, just enjoy the process.

6 Tidy up the thread ends

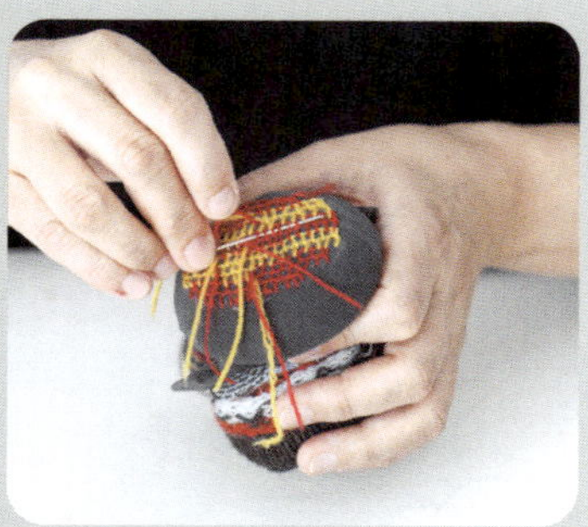

Thread the needle and weave under the stitches for about 2cm (¾in). This should hold as it is, but if you are worried, you can make a knot.

Trim the ends of the threads.

7 Remove tacking (basting)

Remove the elastic and darning mushroom and turn the sock right side (RS) out to cut the basting thread and remove it.

8 Trim off the tights material

Finally, turn the sock WS out so the tights material is accessible.

Trim the tights material along the darning edge with scissors.

Let's darn the other hole

Tip

Darn an area 1–2 cm (3/8–3/4in) larger than the hole. This will help strengthen the surrounding area and make it durable.

Turn the sock WS out, place it on a darning mushroom and tack (baste) a line of stitches 1–2cm (3/8–3/4in) outside the hole.

Place the tights material over the top and apply circular honeycomb stitches (see page 20) inside the line of tacking stitches.

The finished stitching. Tidy up the thread ends, remove tacking and trim excess tights material to finish.

Finished

The parallel honeycomb stitches on the heel look like this from the RS – rows of fine perpendicular stitches.

The circular honeycomb stiches look like fireworks, with stitches worked in all directions.

Work raised seed stitch (see page 26) in undamaged areas just for fun.

If you are not used to sewing, start off with some minor damage first

Yarns and threads for darning

a. Cotton/linen mix, cotton or linen thread

Linen and cotton threads are available as hand-knitting yarn. These often come in a wide range of colours and are suitable for darning. Some yarns can be split into thinner strands.

b. No. 25 embroidery thread

Cotton embroidery thread, or floss, is available in a diverse range of colours. The thread is made up of six super-fine strands that can be split to adjust the thickness. Embroidery thread is not that strong so it may not be suitable for all sock darning.

c. Sashiko thread

Made from 100 per cent cotton, very strong and a little hard to the touch. Thickness and flexibility vary across manufacturers. Readily available online and in crafts shops, so it is easy to acquire.

d. Boucle mohair yarn

Mohair yarn twisted with small loops. Mohair yarn has good elasticity and breathability and is most suitable for darning. Chunky boucle (right) is good for the heels of thick socks, and thin boucle (left) is recommended for all socks.

e. Wool/silk mix

This yarn is made with silk fibre twisted with wool. It's easy to stitch as it is not as slippery as a silk thread. Stronger than a normal wool-mix yarn and recommended for silk sock lovers.

f. Cashmere yarn

Can be used for socks made from all materials, not just cashmere. Supple and smooth to touch, warm and richly textured.

g. Wool embroidery thread

Wool embroidery threads are sold in crafts shops and online. They come in a wide range of colours so they are suitable when you're looking for nuanced colours.

h. British wool

Super elastic and warm, popular yarn for hand-knitted socks. These yarns shrink slowly with washing, and gradually felt to fit the foot shape, leading to an effect similar to that of shoe insoles.

Strength and durability are not the only factors: colour and texture are important things to consider too

In darning, there is no rule about which yarn fibre should be used. Natural fibres have great texture, synthetic fibres are durable, there are advantages to each; choose them to match the sock.

i. Acrylic yarn

Acrylic yarn, used for knitting and handcraft, is readily available in a broad range of colours. Texture and durability vary depending on use or wash, but they can be used as 'almighty' threads for sock darning.

j. Button thread

Durable strong thread. Plenty of colours and useful when you need a definitive colour. It's great for darning denim but does not give a finish soft enough for socks. Recommended when you need strength.

k. Sock yarn

The recent popularity of hand-knit socks has led to a rich variety of wool yarn designed especially. This blended yarn has a good texture and is often mixed with synthetics, such as nylon or polyester, for strength.

l. Synthetic thread

Polyester and nylon thread is used for sewing stretchy clothes such as swimming costumes or leotards. It is similar to the heel thread for socks (see page 2) or the thread used for tights, it produces a smooth touch and firm reinforcement. They are highly elastic threads and so it can be hard to handle until you are familiar with it. Also, if your fingertips are dry, fine fibres may snag; use hand cream to moisturize. This thread is super susceptible to tangling, so use a maximum of 50cm (20in) lengths.

How to combine threads

It is good to combine weak cotton embroidery threads with durable synthetic threads.

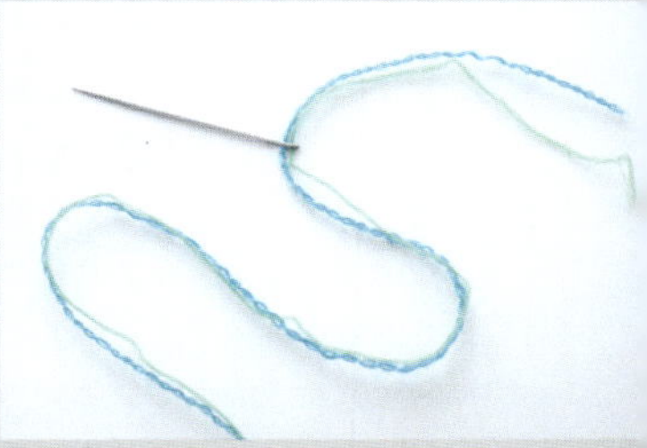

How to divide thread

To match the thickness of the sock, you can divide the thread. Cut a 50cm (20in) length and divide from the centre by gently teasing the individual threads apart.

* Dividing will reduce the strength of the thread. Check the strength before using.

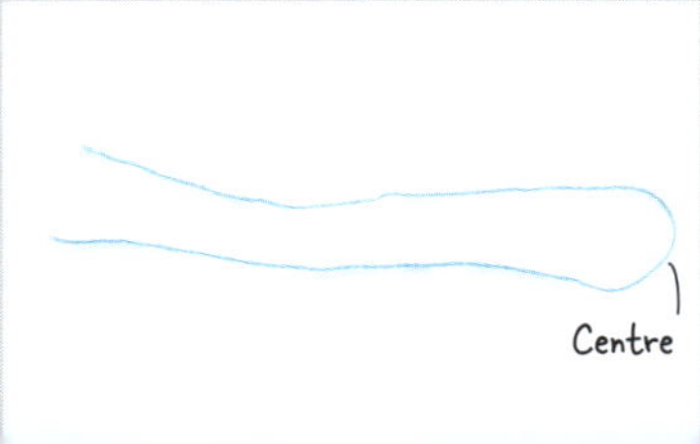

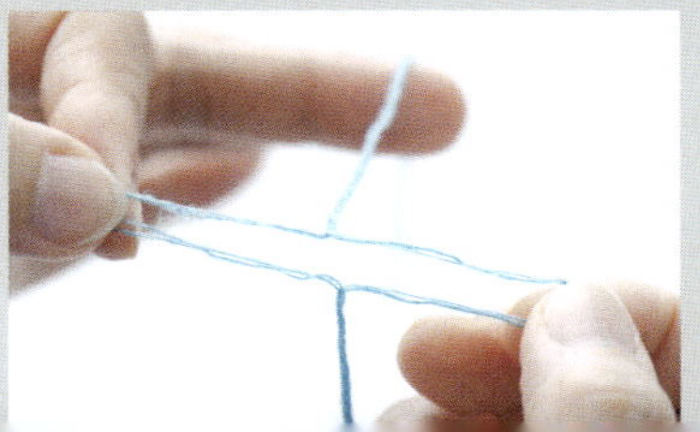

Tools for darning

A darning mushroom, needles, threads and scissors are essential. Introduced below are the tools that are useful when darning.

1. Darning mushroom *
A mushroom-shaped tool specifically for darning. Very useful for sock darning.

2. Darning stick *
For use when darning the toes on five-toe socks.

3. Darning disc *
Good for darning long socks or tights. Its shape makes it easy to insert and take out.

4. Darning jellyfish *
Its low centre of gravity provides extra stability when darning. Most suitable for sock darning.

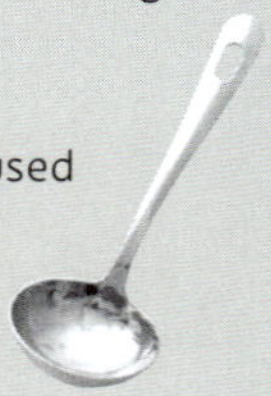

Ladle

The head/end of the ladle can be used for darning.

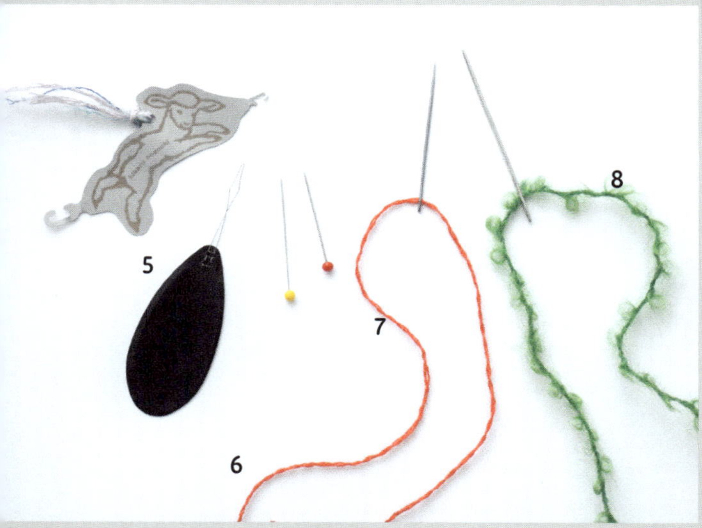

5. Hook-type threader *
A tool for threading needles. Use the hook to pick up the thread.

6. Wire-type threader
Another type of needle threader. This one is used by putting the wire through the eye of the needle.

7. Pins
Useful when temporarily fixing materials or threads.

8. Needles
A darning needle (left) or French embroidery needle No. 3. With a thick yarn, use a blunt knitter's needle, or a tapestry embroidery needle (right).

Tailors' chalk – use for drawing guidelines on socks. Can be erased easily by hand.

Ruler – for drawing guidelines etc. It's useful to have one around.

Tacking (basting) thread – pre-cut lengths. To temporarily fix patches on socks.

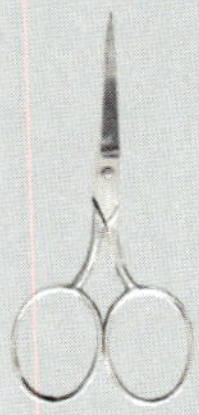

Thread cutting scissors – small and sharp.

Fabric shears – for cutting fabric only!

* Original tools for darning by Hikaru Noguchi.

How to thread a needle

You can thread a needle with or without a threader, which can be either a wire type or a hook type.

Get your fingers ready by opening and closing your fingertips.

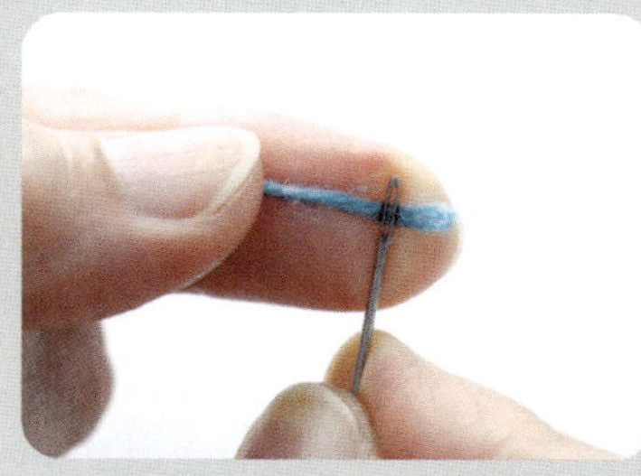

1 Place the thread end on your index finger and put the side of the needle eye on top.

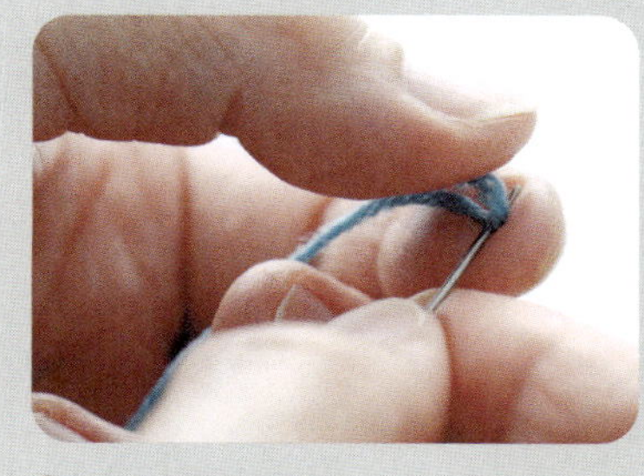

2 Fold the thread in half where the needle is and squeeze with your thumb and index finger.

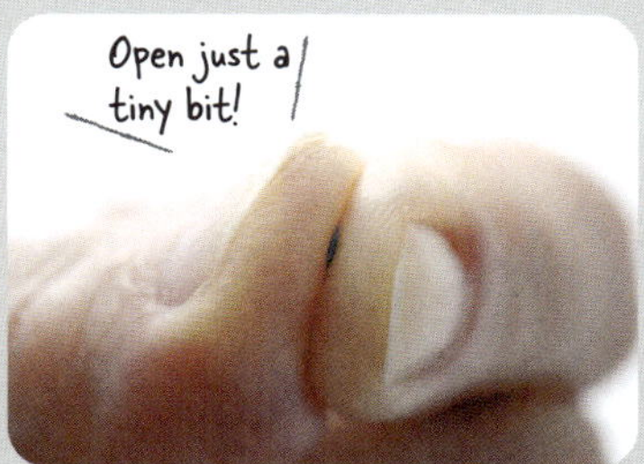

3 Remove the needle gently and open your fingertips until you can see the fold of the thread.

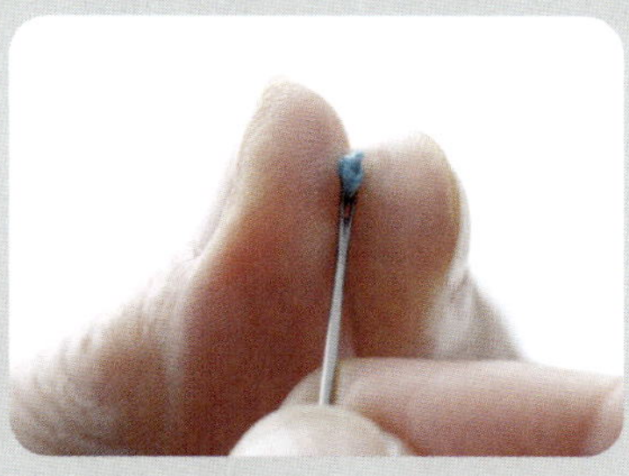

4 Keeping the position in step 3, put the needle eye on the fold of the thread, and gently open the fingertips to thread the needle.

5 The fold has just gone through the needle eye. Pull in the direction of the arrow.

How to use threaders

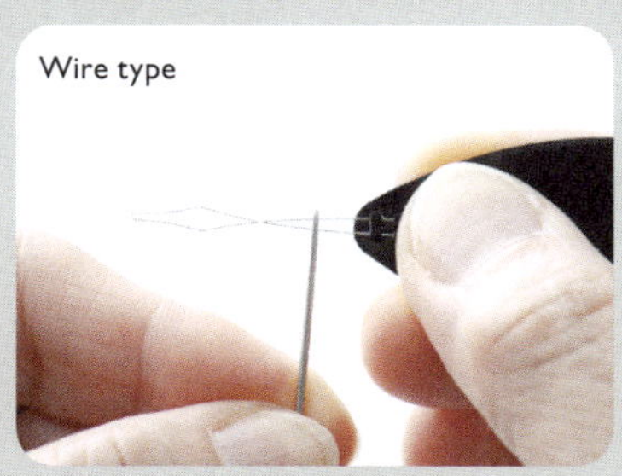

1 Push the wire section through the eye of the needle.

2 Put the thread through the wire.

3 Pull the threader, with thread, through the eye of the needle. When pulling, make sure you hold the section where the wire is attached.

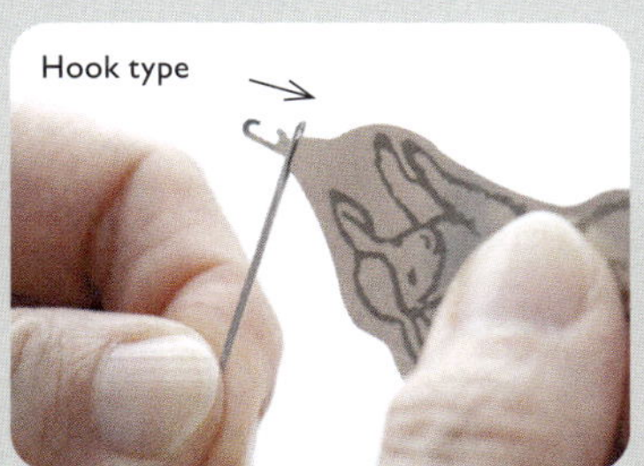

1 Put the hook through the eye of the needle.

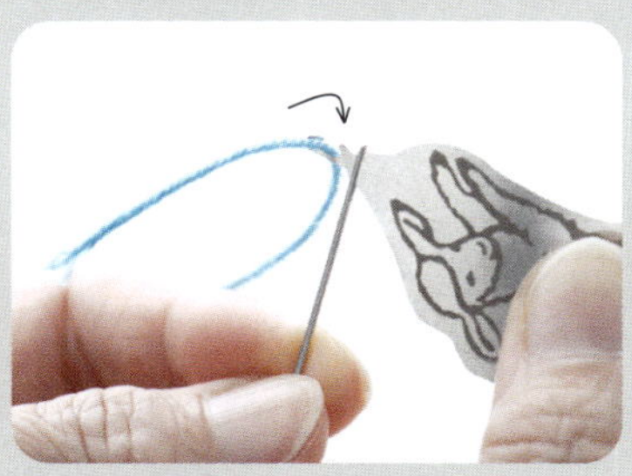

2 Hook the thread.

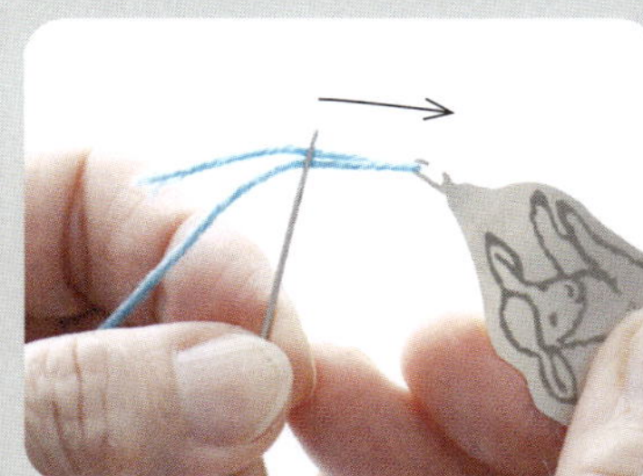

3 Pull the threader, and thread, through the eye of the needle.

Saviour of sock darning:

Hosiery

As a reinforcing material for sock darning, tights are invaluable. Their elasticity fits the sock, and even a large hole can be easily darned. For minor or heavy thinning damage reinforcement with tights enhances durability.

Tights material makes sock darning much easier!

Materials for reinforcing socks

1 Tights – very fine tights could be used doubled up.

2 Thick winter tights – suitable for warm and hand-knit socks.

3 Grey knee-highs – grey is versatile and matches lots of colours.

4 Sheer material socks – socks made from sheer elastic fabric can be used too.

5 Nylon or polyester mesh – very fine fabrics with elasticity and transparency.

Put it on a darning mushroom!

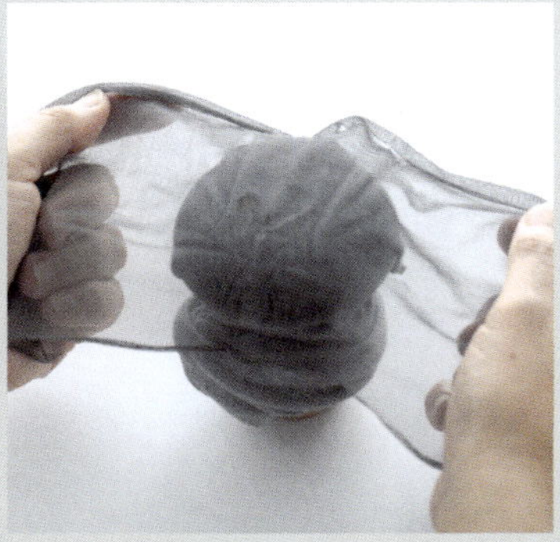

Cut the tights material into a square and place it gently on the sock, which is on the darning mushroom, with the centre on top of the damaged area. The key is not to pull or stretch.

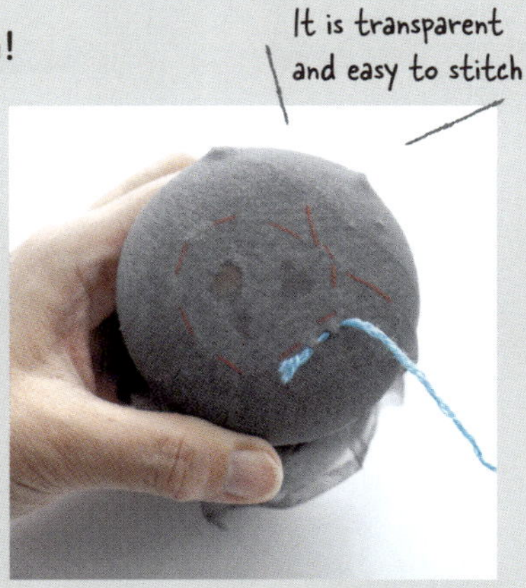

Secure with a rubber band and start stitching where the patch is layered on top of the sock (see page 16).

Using tights with a darning stick

The cut tights square is put on a darning stick and then pushed inside a sock (see page 17).

Different ways of using tights

It's recommended to darn using tights material for worn areas as well as for holes. Different methods apply depending on whether you are darning from the right side (RS) or wrong side (WS) of the sock fabric, and if you are using non-transparent tights material.

A: Darning from the RS of the sock

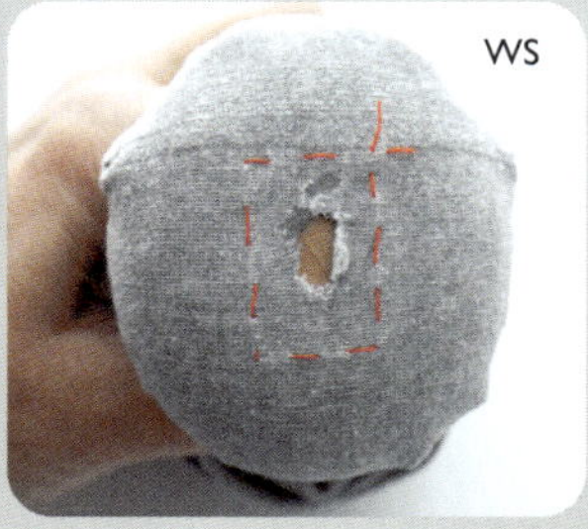

Turn the sock WS out, place on the darning mushroom and secure it with a rubber band. Tack (baste) around the darning area, 1–2cm (3/8–3/4in) outside of the hole.

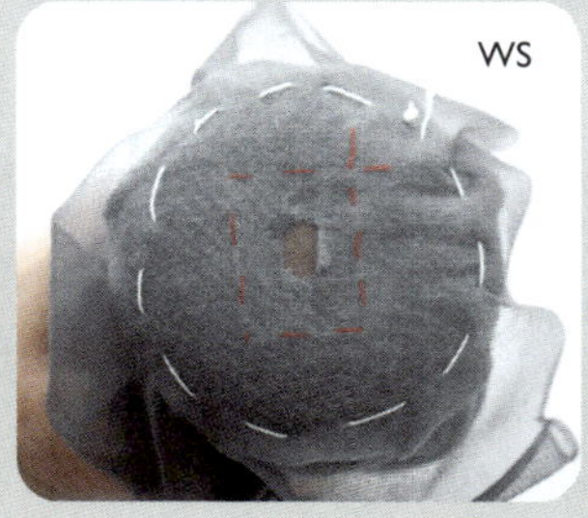

Position the tights material gently over the hole, use tacking stitches around the area to secure. If you are repairing a hole, use two layers, for a thinned area, use just one layer.

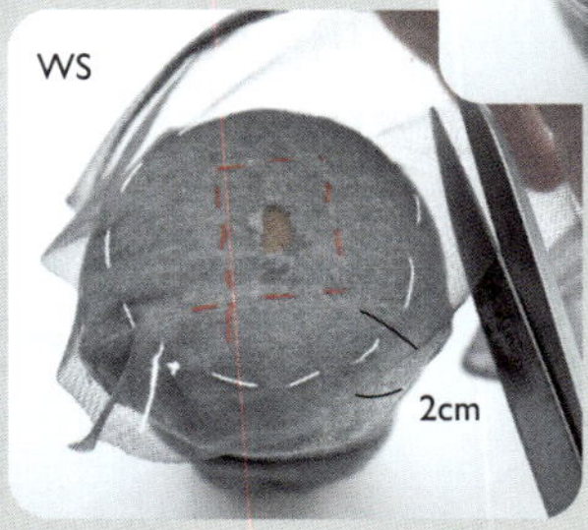

Trim the tights material down to 2cm (3/4in) outside the tacking stitches. Remove the darning mushroom, turn the sock RS out, place it back on the mushroom and secure with an elastic.

Darn inside the tacking stitches from the RS

B: Darning from the WS of the sock

Follow the same method as for A as far as the tacking.

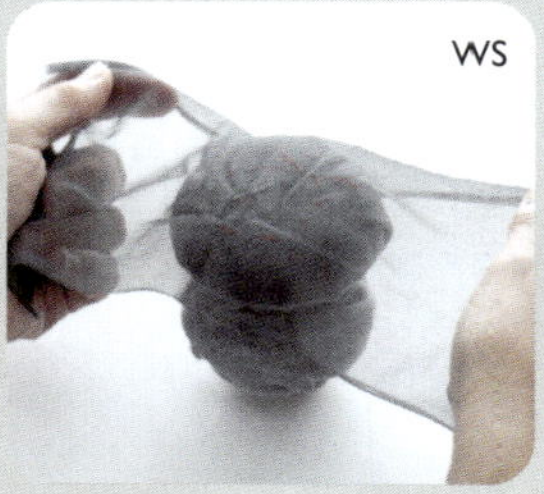

Place the tights material on top of the hole. Two layers are recommended for a hole, one for a thinned area.

Wrap with a rubber band to secure.

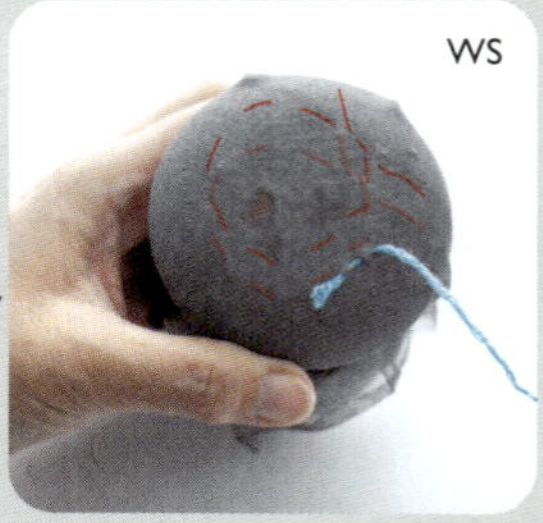

Darn inside the tacking stitches from the WS.

C: Using non-transparent tights materials

Place the tights material on the darning mushroom, wrap a rubber band around it twice to secure.

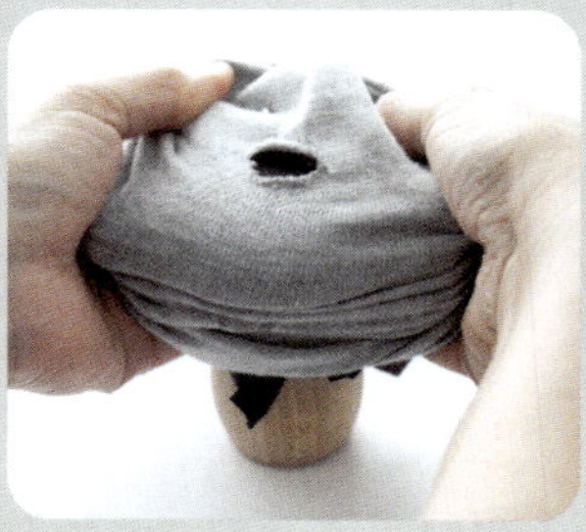

Turn the sock WS out and put it on the mushroom.

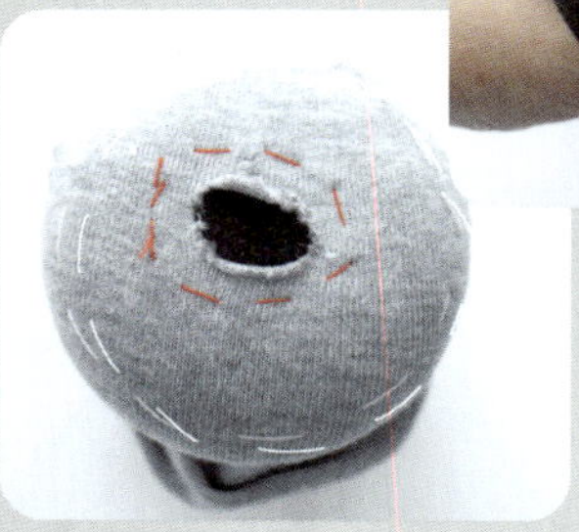

Secure with a band and tack around the area to be darned. If you are darning from the RS, darn inside the tacked line as it is. If you want to darn from the WS, tack around the mushroom and then turn the sock WS out.

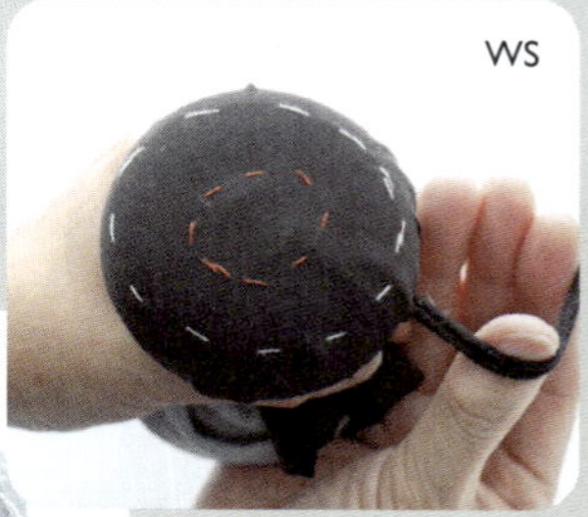

If you are darning from the WS, the tacking (red) shows where the hole is.

Areas most susceptible to damage

Damage occurs differently depending on the wearer, but there are several areas of socks most susceptible to damage.

Sock opening

Elasticated opening becomes loose over time. It is possible to fix it by using a new elastic thread. If the elastic is too tight, you can also fix it. See p27 for repairing.

Heel/back

The back of the heel, close to the Achilles tendon, can be a high friction area. Check it routinely so that you can darn while it is only lightly thinned.

Toe tips

Toe tips also get damaged through friction of the toenails. It is a narrow space, so it requires skill to apply the darning mushroom.

Heel/sole

The bottom of the heel gets even higher friction than the back. The damage occurs in a wide area, so it is worth stitching a little more widely.

Ball

The area at the base of the toes, the rounded area like a cat's paw. When you walk, you kick through this area, so it is likely to be damaged.

Toe pads

You often notice holes around the toe pads. Five-toe socks are typically damaged on the toe pads. In such a case, use a darning stick to repair.

Using a darning stick for five-toe socks

→

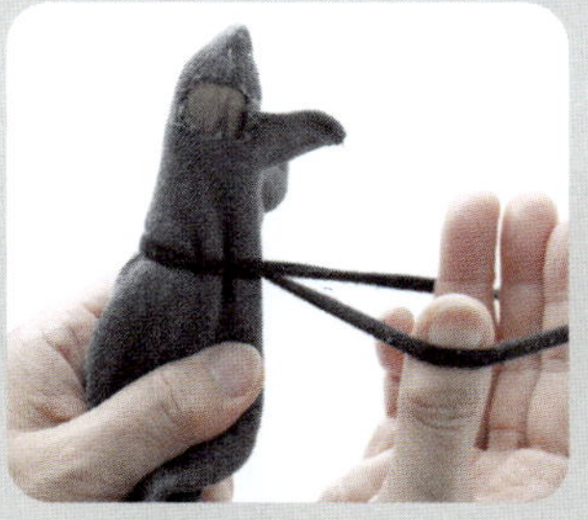

Place a 15cm (5¾in) square piece of tights material on the stick and secure with a rubber band. Insert the stick into the toe of the sock, add another rubber band and then darn.

Tips for using the mushroom for toe tips

The tip of the sock will not flatten when placed on top of the mushroom. Pull to flatten the area as shown in the photo.

Technique 1

Parallel honeycomb stitch

This darning method works by applying blanket stitches in parallel horizontal lines, working from the bottom. It looks good from the RS or WS. In this example, it was stitched from the WS. There is no need to match up all the stitches of the rows tidily – just darn without worrying. No need for tights material for minor damage, such as thinning.

Stitching start

* In this example, the tights material and stitches are applied from the WS.

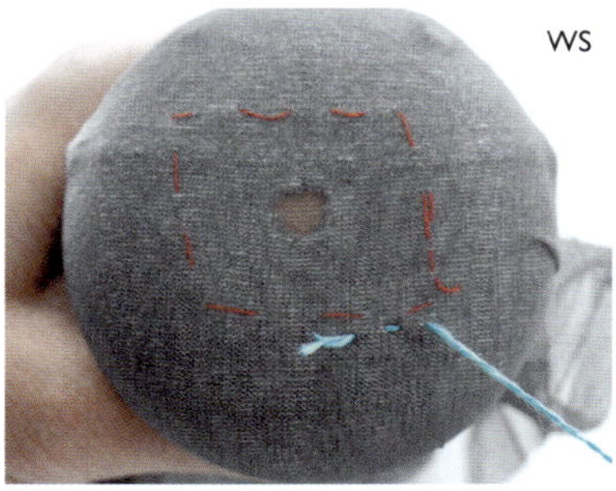

1 See B on page 16 and place on the darning mushroom. Start 2cm (3/4in) left of the bottom right-hand corner and work two running stitches (see page 28).

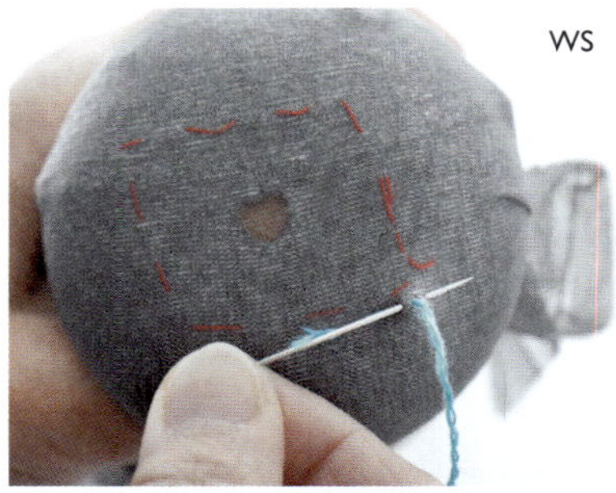

2 Go back about 1mm (1/16in) and stitch the material – this will set the start of the darning.

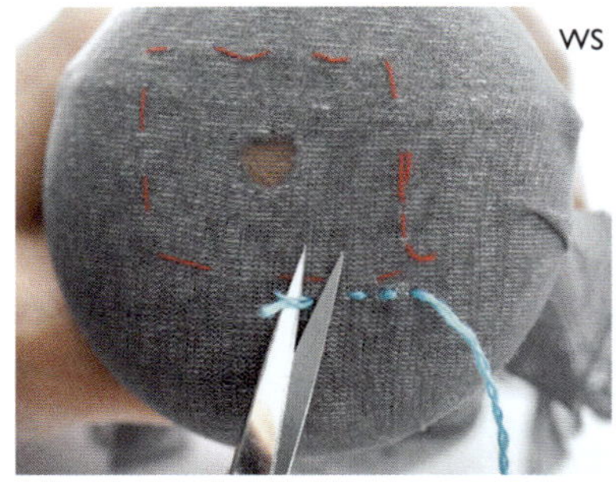

3 Trim the tail end of the thread.

Parallel honeycomb stitch

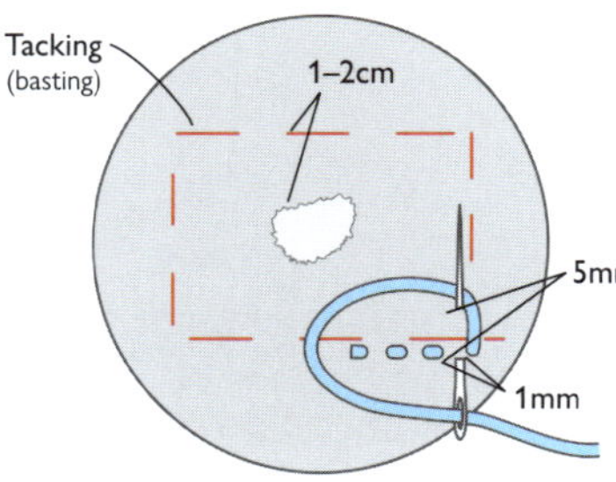

4 Insert the needle about 1mm (1/16in) to the left, bring it out 5mm (1/4in) above, wrapping the thread around the needle from right to left.

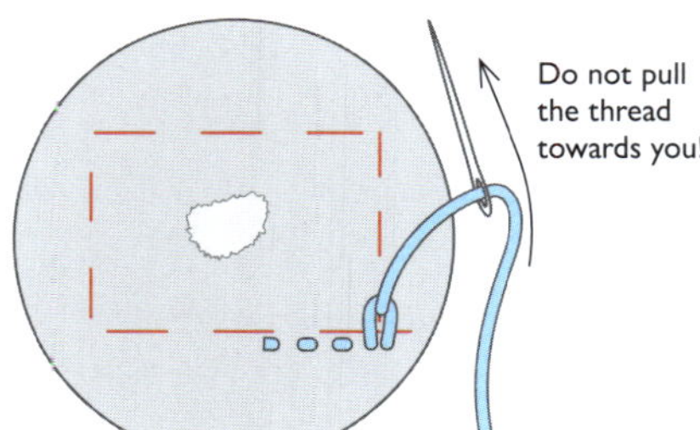

5 Pull the thread lightly. Pull gently and pull away from you, not towards you.

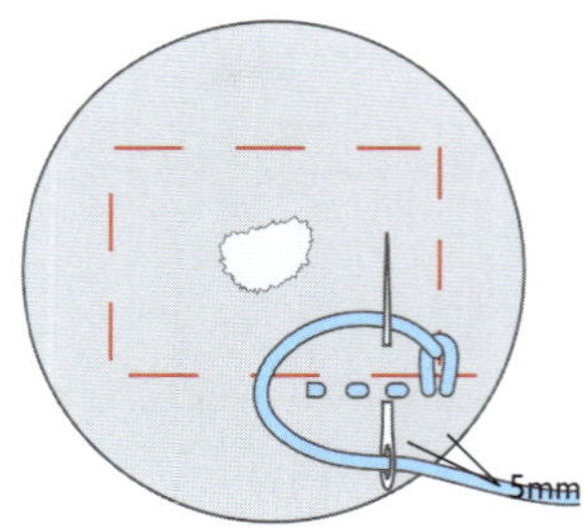

6 Insert the needle about 5mm (1/4in) to the left, bring out 5mm (1/4in) above, wrapping the thread from right to left around the needle. If you keep the thread to the left side, this will happen naturally and smoothly. Repeat steps 4 and 5 to finish the row.

Starting the second row

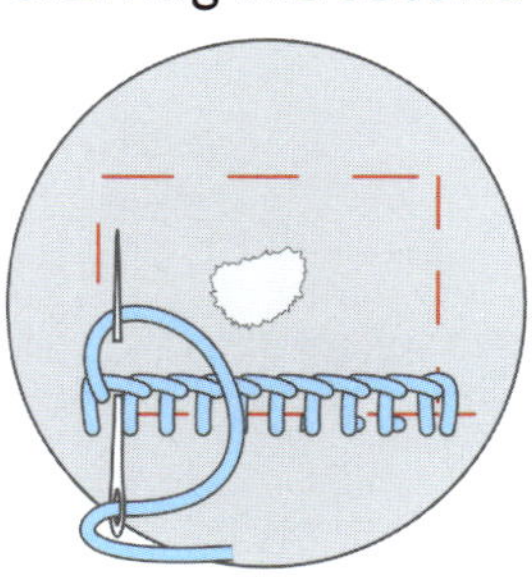

7 When the first row is finished, start a new row. Insert the needle close to where it came out, and bring it out 5mm (1/4in) above. Wrap the thread from left to right, and stitch to the right.

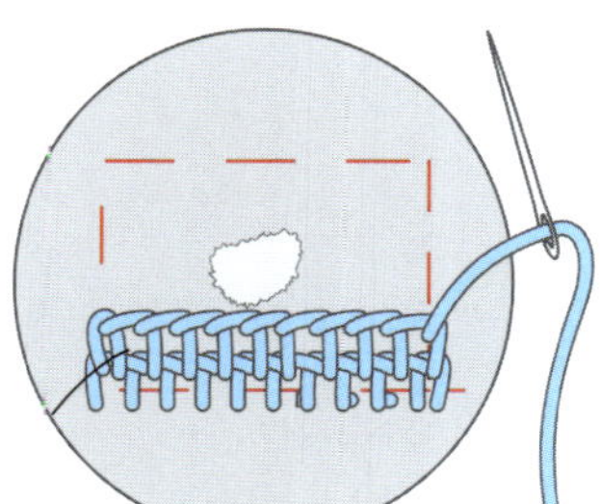

8 The second row is done. The first stitch of the second row looks like a chain.

Tip

Insert the needle until you can feel the hard surface of the mushroom. This is the evidence that you are stitching the material and the sock together.

THREADS USED:

Acrylic wool yarn (blue, pink)
*split for use.

Changing the thread

9 When you only have a small amount of thread left, remove it from the needle and use a new colour of thread (pink) to continue, wrapping the old (blue) thread and pulling the new (pink) one. Bring the ends of both threads together and secure with a pin or masking tape until you have finished. Continue with the new thread.

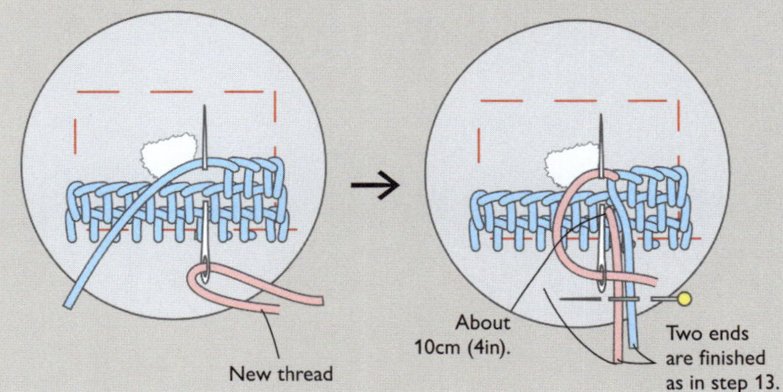

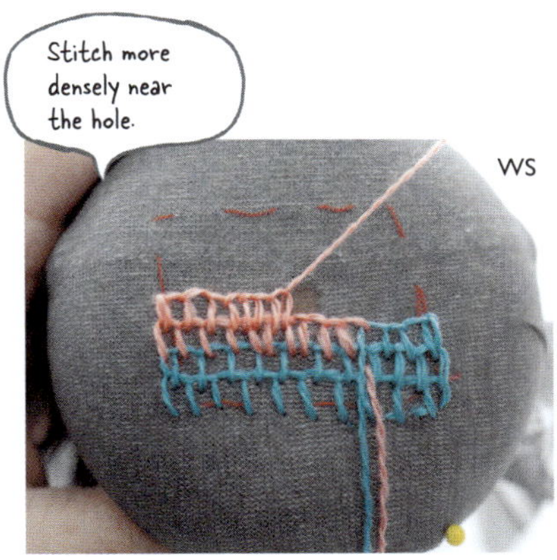

10 Make the stitches finer for the area around the hole but take care not to pull too hard!

End of stitching

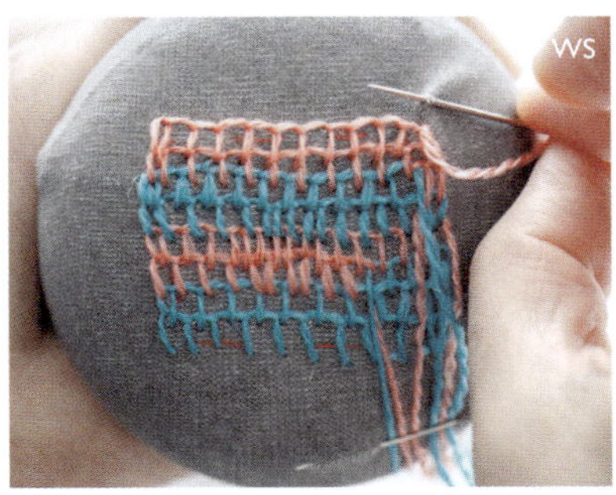

11 When all rows are finished, make a small stitch at the right-hand corner.

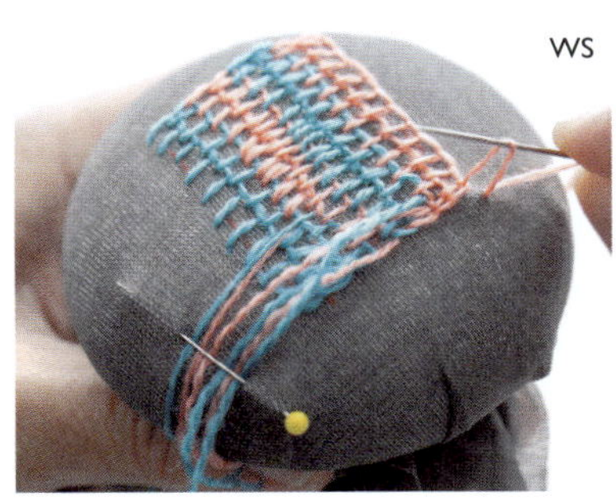

12 After working a small stitch, put the needle under the working thread and pull to hold it firmly.

Finishing thread ends

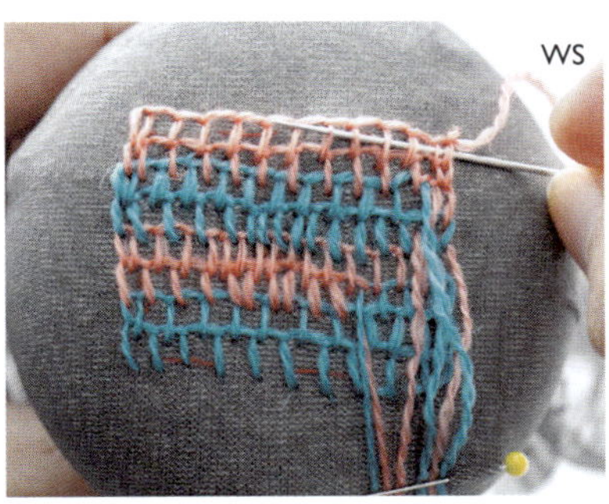

13 Finish the thread on the WS. Pull the thread end beneath the darned stitches for about 2cm (¾in) and cut.

Finished – take out the tacking stitches, trim the tights material and turn RS out.

RS

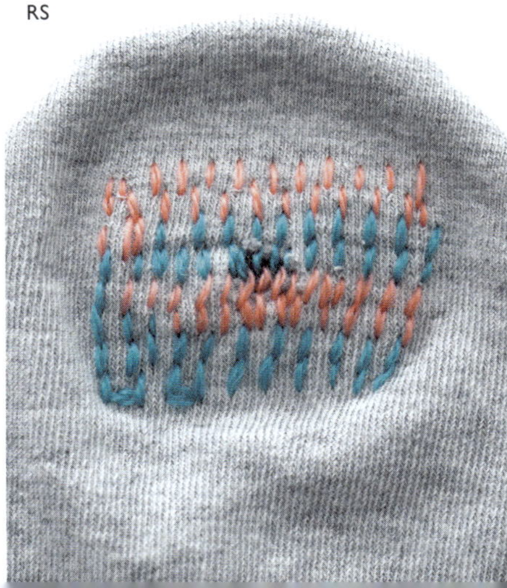

WS

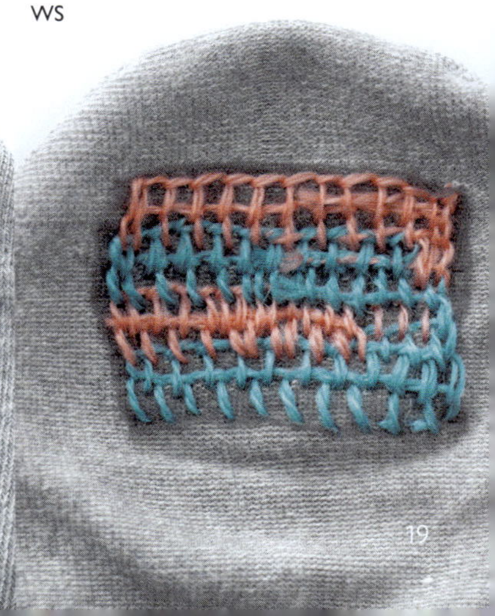

Technique 2

Circular honeycomb stitch

Work honeycomb stitches in a circular pattern. This is a great technique to use on heavily thinned areas or holes. It gives elasticity and feels good to touch. The RS looks like honeycomb, the WS gives a pattern like fireworks.

Stitching start

* In this example, a sock with a hole is turned WS out, tights material is applied and it is darned from the WS.

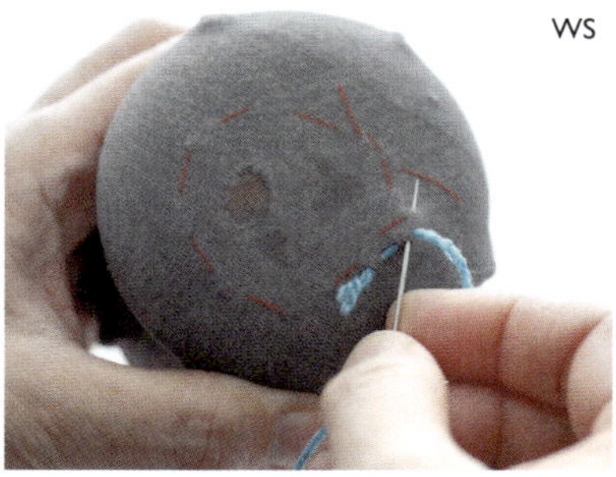

1 Set up the darning mushroom according to B on page 16. Work running stitch just outside the tacked line and then go back about 1mm (1/16in) and make a stitch.

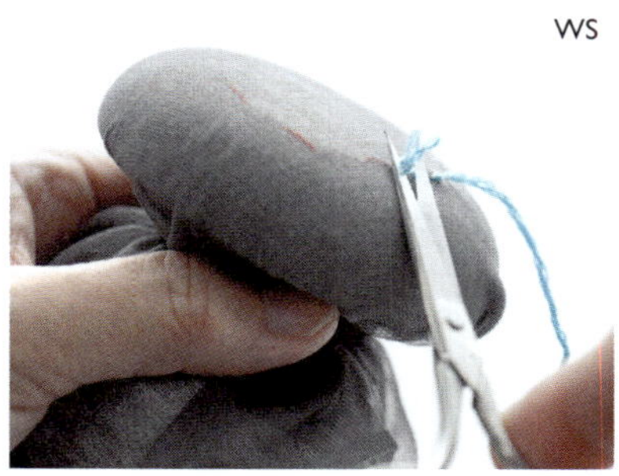

2 Cut off the thread tail from the first stitch.

Tip

Do not pull the thread too much!

Honeycomb stitches are usually 0.5–1cm (3/16–3/8in) but you can choose the stitch size you like. It is also not necessary to keep the stitches aligned. The only thing to bear in mind is not to pull the thread too tightly as that will make the stitched areas hard.

Working circular honeycomb stitch

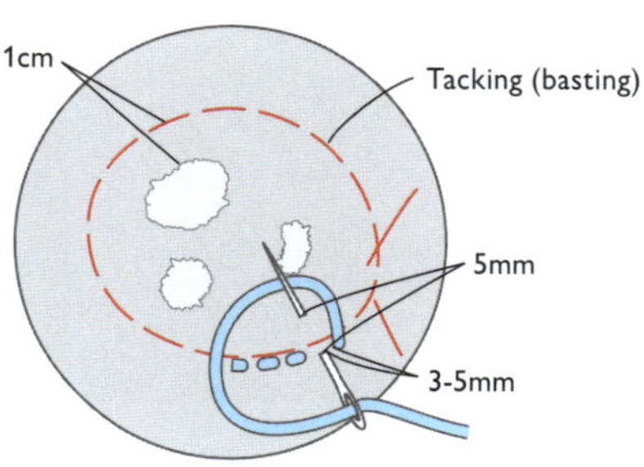

3 Insert the needle 3–5mm (1/8–1/4in) to the left and bring it out 5mm (1/4in) above. Wrap the thread around the needle as shown in the illustration from right to left.

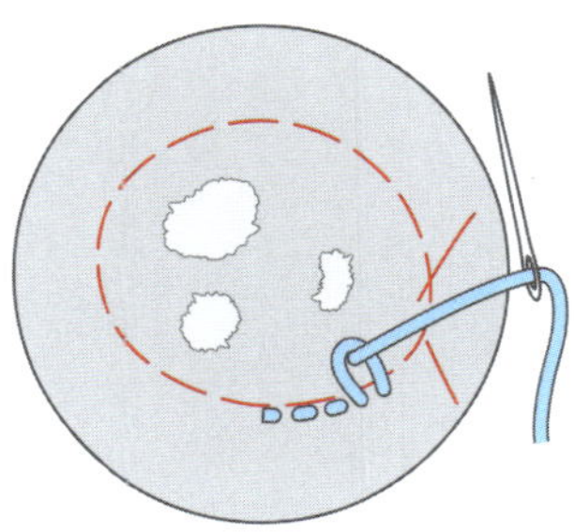

4 Pull the needle lightly. When you pull, do not pull towards you, pull away from you.

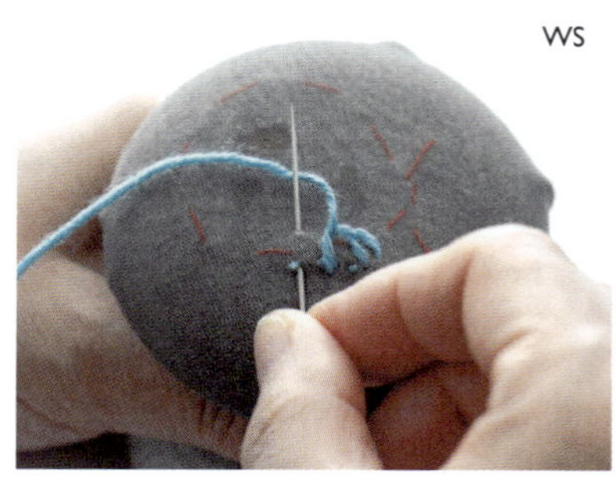

5 Working along the tacked line, stitch in the same way as for parallel honeycomb stitch (see page 18).

Changing the thread

6 When you only have a small amount of thread left, remove it from the needle and use a new colour (pink) to continue, wrapping the old (blue) thread. Bring the ends of both threads together and secure with a pin or masking tape. Continue with the new thread.

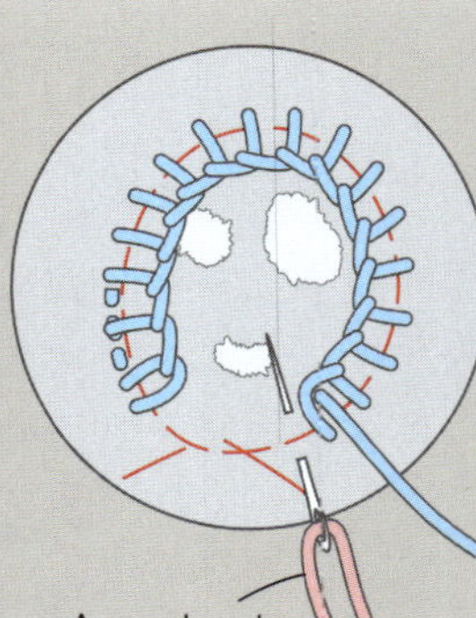

→

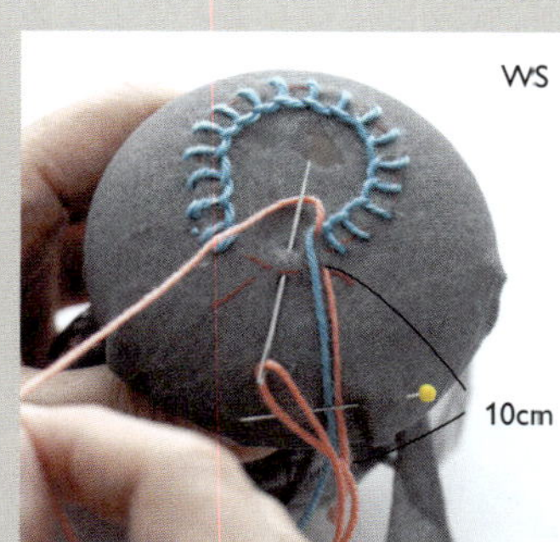

THREADS USED:
acrylic yarn (blue and pink)

Starting the second row

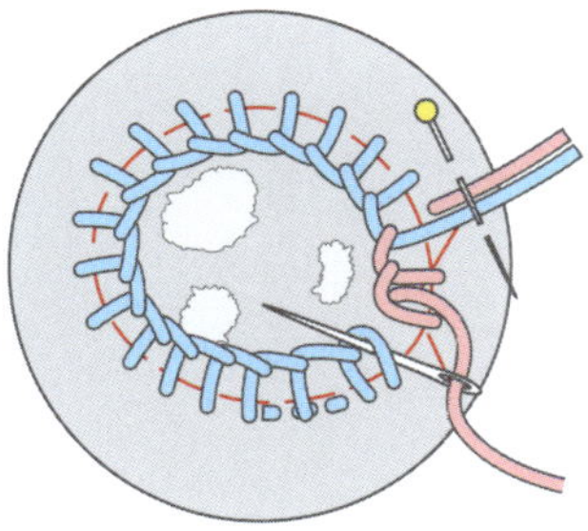

7 When the first row is finished, pass the needle under the first stitch. This is the end of the first row.

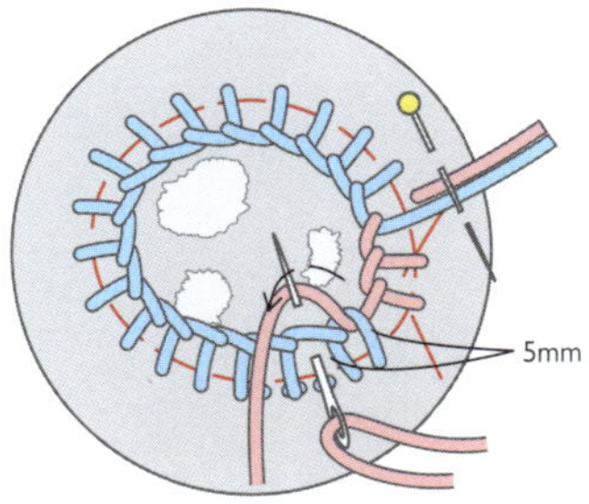

8 For the second row, move about 5mm (¼in) to the left, insert the needle a little below the first-row thread and bring it out 5mm (¼in) above. Wrap the thread from the right to left and pull.

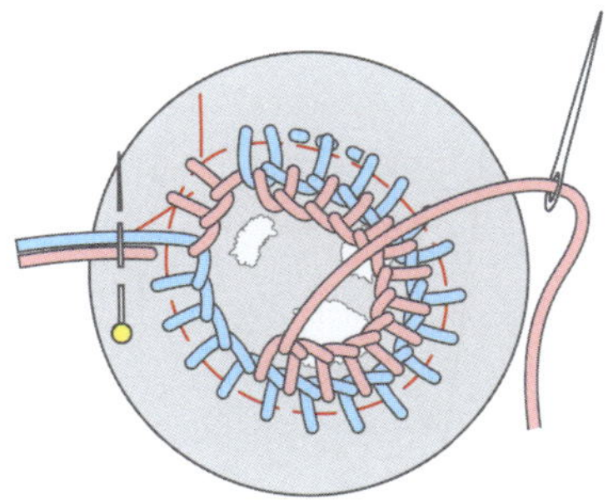

9 The second row of stitches does not need to have the same number of stitches as the first, just keep on stitching 5mm (¼in) to the left.

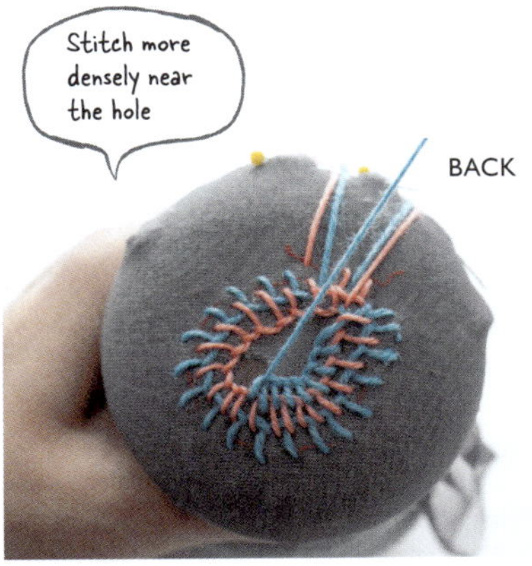

10 Make the stitches finer for the area around the hole but take care not to pull too hard! This area can become stiff with too many dense stitches.

End of stitches

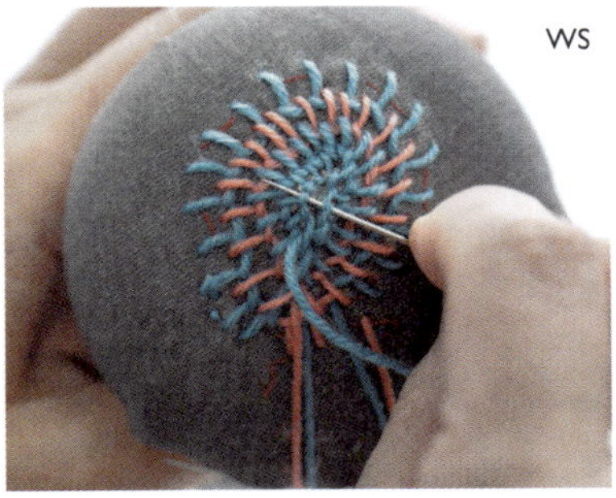

11 When you have finished stitching to the centre, pass the needle through threads on both sides to close it off.

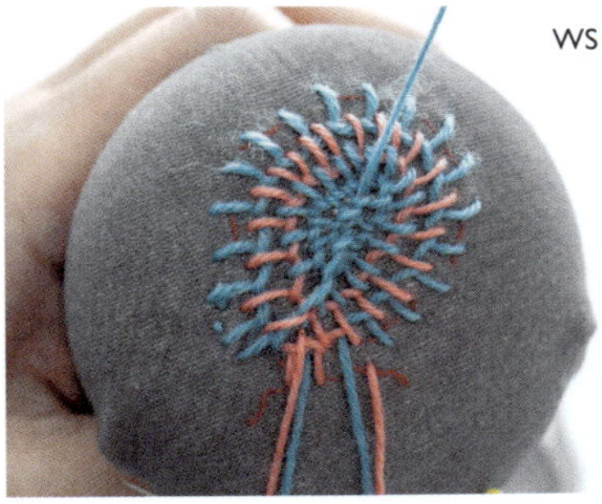

12 This is how it looks after you have closed off.

Finishing ends

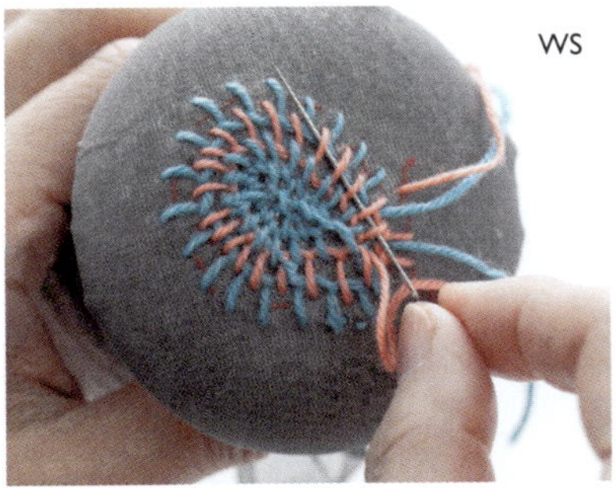

13 Weave the remaining thread ends through 2cm (¾in) of stitches and then cut. You can weave a couple of thread ends at the same time.

The darning is finished. Cut the tacking away and trim the tights material. If the tights material is too visible, apply more honeycomb stitches from the RS.

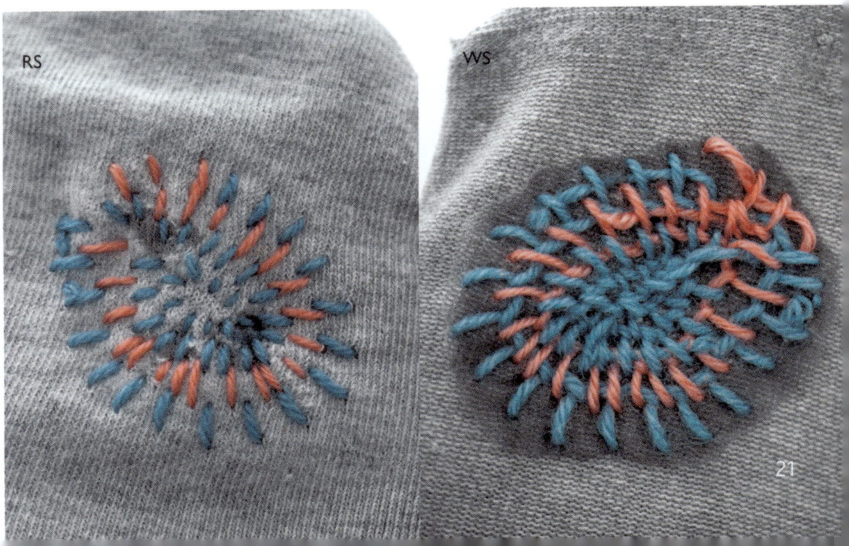

Technique 3

Seed stitch

These small stitches look like sesame seeds, hence the name. It is elastic and robust with dense threads at the back as it is a variation of backstitch. Applying stitches from two directions makes it extra durable.

Two-directional seed stitch

* In this example, the sock with a hole is WS out, covered with the tights material and stitched from the WS.

1 Prepare your needles by threading them with two different threads: blue woolly yarn and yellow-green cashmere yarn.

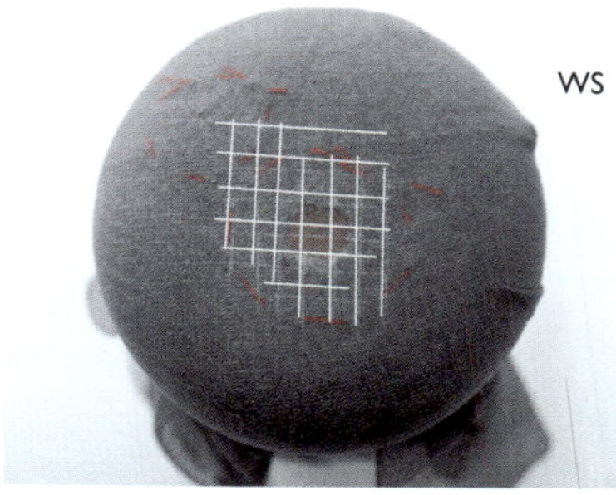

2 Place on the darning mushroom according to B on page 16. Use chalk to mark the grid with 0.5–1cm (¼in–⅜in) intervals if you like.

Use guidelines if you want to.

Two-way seed stitches are easier to work if you mark a grid guideline, but it is not essential. Even if the lines are not neat, it can still look tasteful.

First, stitch horizontally for two rows

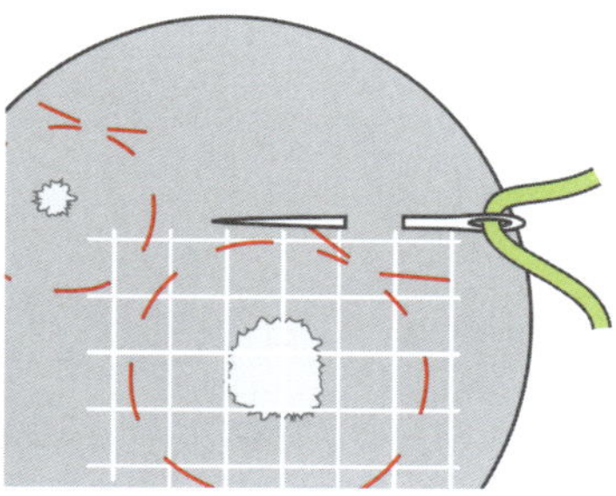

3 Start stitching at the top right using yellow-green thread. Go 1cm (⅜in) from right to left.

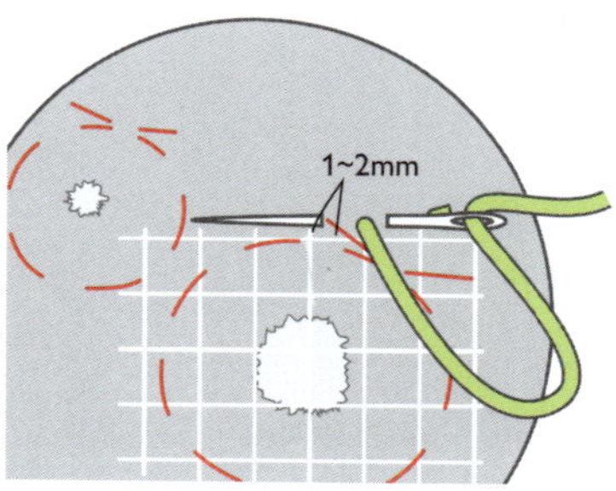

4 Next, insert the needle a sesame seed length (1–2mm [approx. 1/16in]) back and bring it out 0.5–1cm (¼in–⅜in) in front.

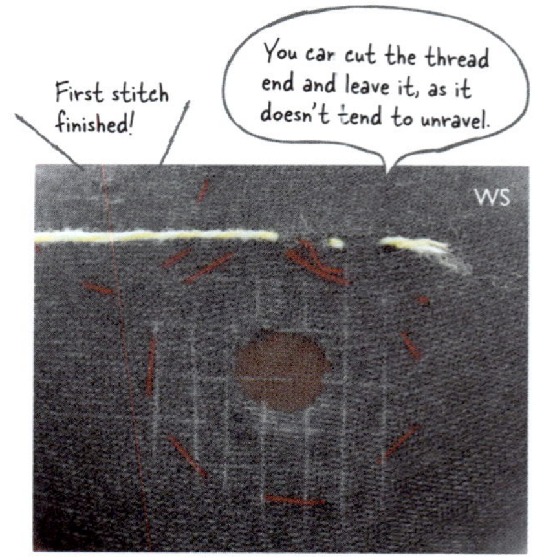

5 When you pull the thread, the first seed stitch is done. Repeat the process and continue to stitch along the line.

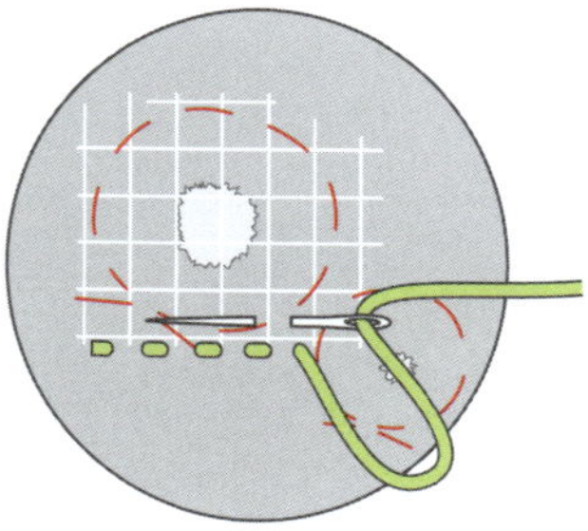

6 When the first row is finished, turn the darning mushroom by 180 degrees and work the second row in the same way. It is not necessary for the second row stitches to match the first row.

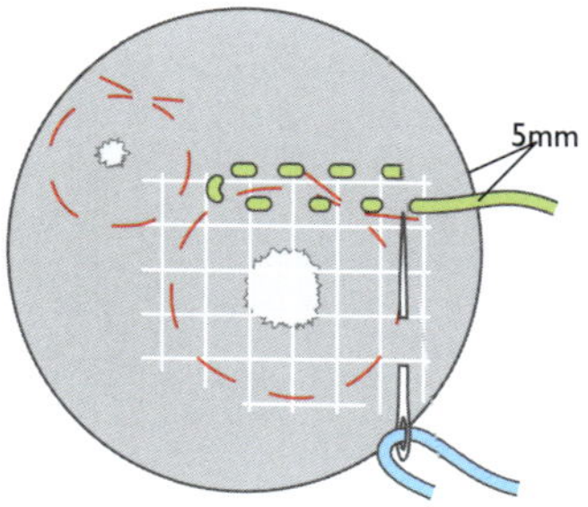

7 When the second horizontal row is finished, start the vertical rows. Insert the needle with blue thread at the bottom right and bring it out about 1cm (⅜in) above.

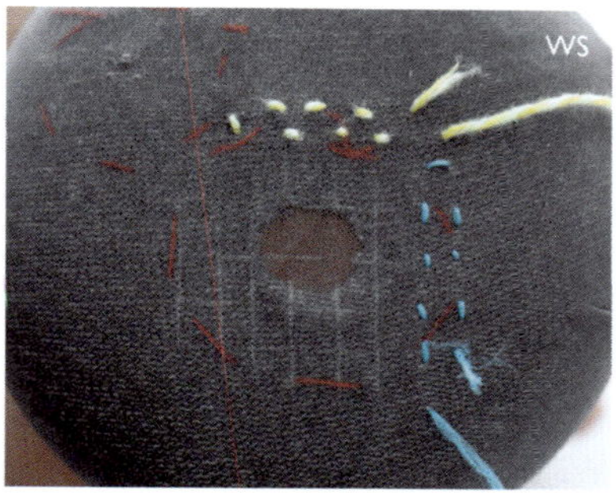

8 Stitch using the same method as for steps 4–6 for two vertical rows.

THREADS USED:

Woolly yarn (blue)
cashmere yarn (yellow green)

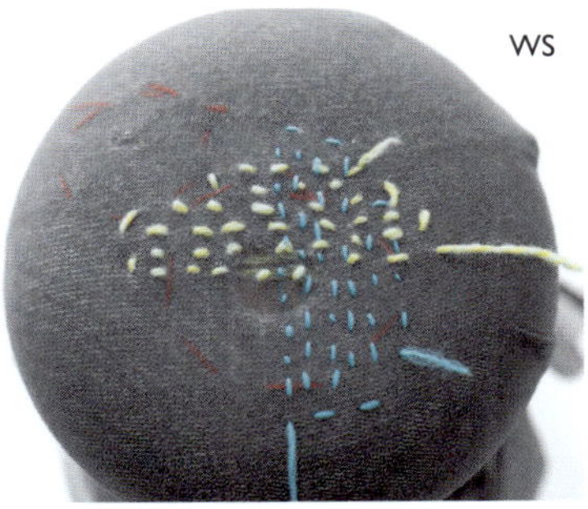

9 Work two rows each of horizontal yellow-green stitches and vertical blue stitches alternately.

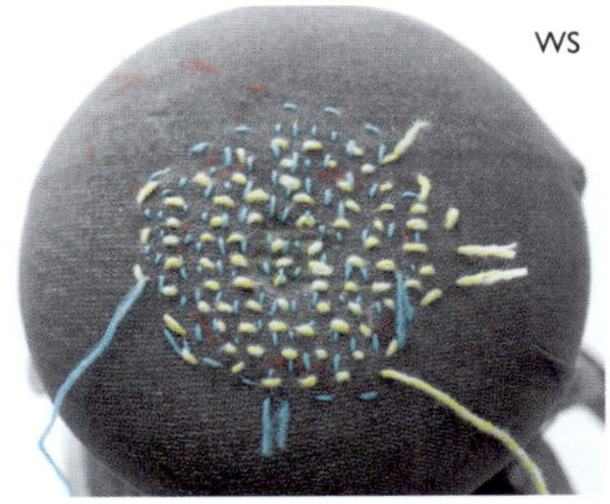

10 This is how it looks when you finish stitching.

Finishing ends

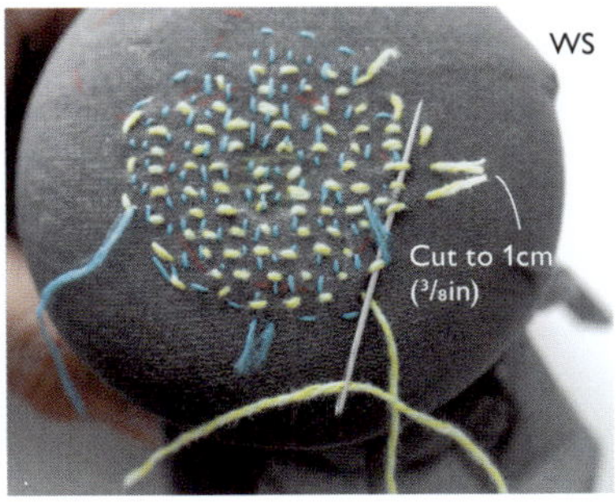

11 To fasten off, you can just cut the end leaving a 1cm (3/8in) tail, but if you are worried, pass the needle through 2cm (3/4in) of stitches to secure.

Basic seed stitch (one direction seed stitch)

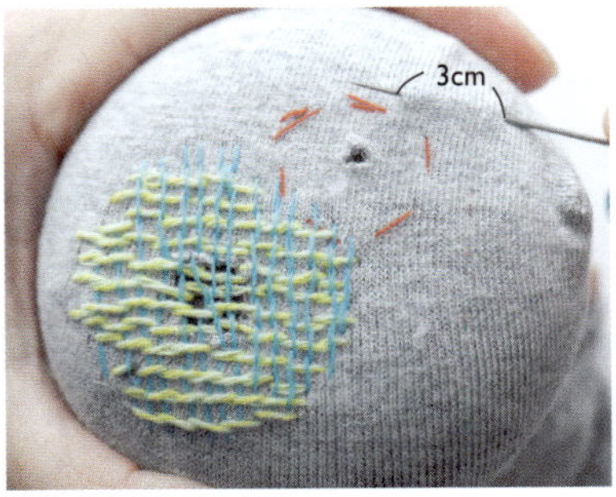

1 Turn the sock RS out and place it on the darning mushroom. Insert the needle about 3cm (1¼in) outside the tacking (basting) at the top right of the hole and bring it out just by the tacking.

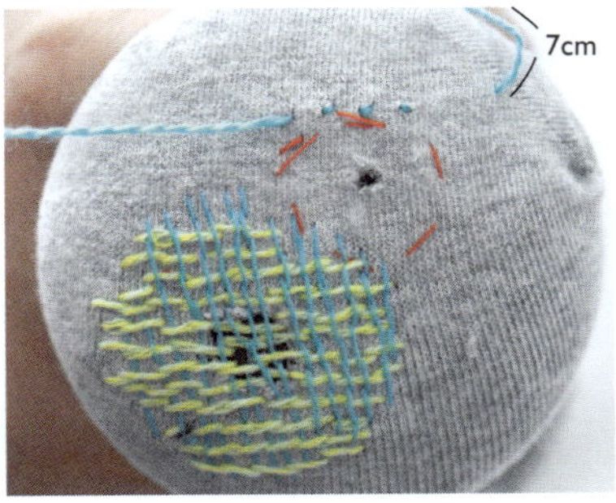

2 Pull the thread through and leave a 7cm (2¾in) tail. Work seed stitches from right to left.

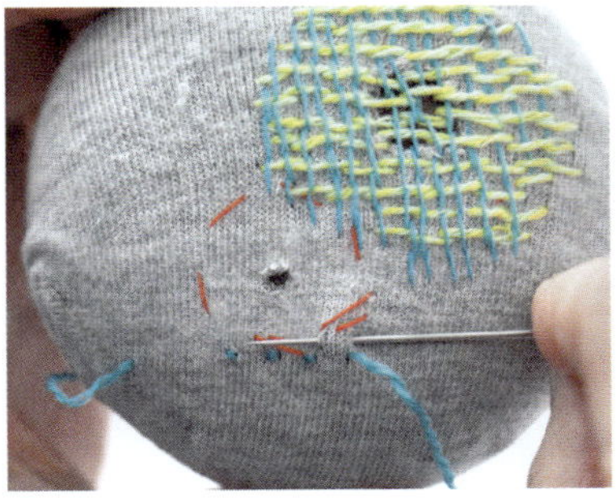

3 After the first row, turn the darning mushroom by 180 degrees, and stitch the second row. Repeat steps 3–4 of two-directional seed stitch (see page 22).

Finished

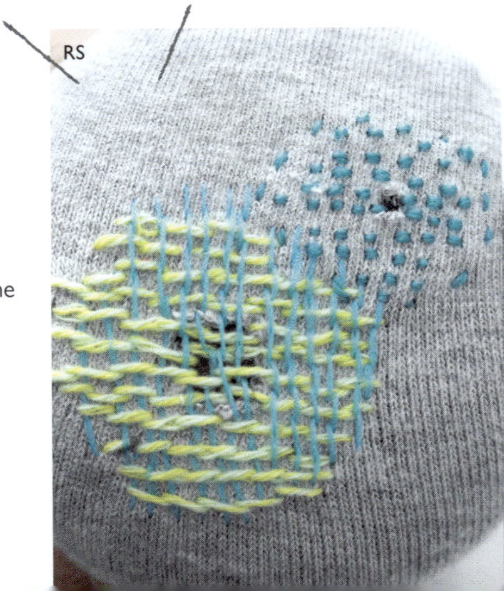

Thread ends should be brought to the WS and cut. Remove the tacking, trim the tights material and it's done. When you use two colours for horizontal stitches and two colours for vertical stitches it gives a complex appearance a little like weaving (see page 65).

Technique 4

English basket darning

A familiar method in darning, basket darning (sometimes called basketweave) creates a surface with warp and weft threads. For sock darning, English basket darning, where you incorporate the sock material, is recommended

Warp

* In this example, the sock with a hole is fitted with the tights material from the WS and stitched from the RS.

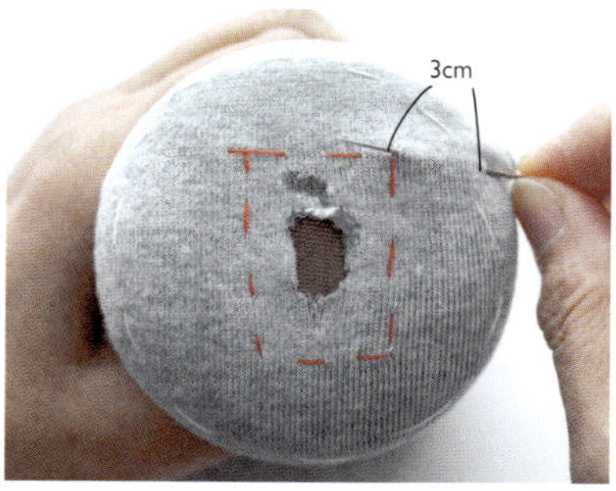

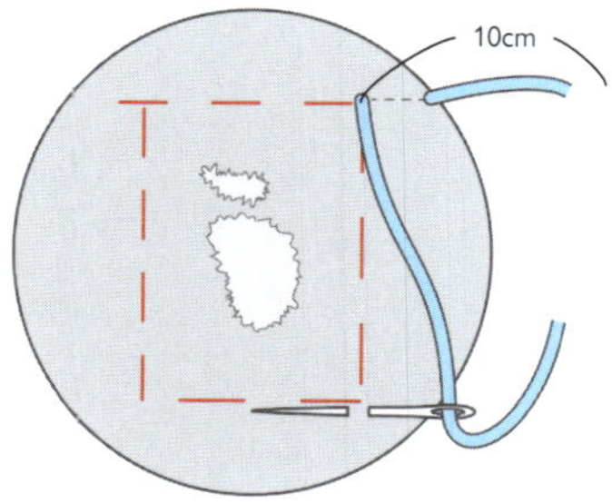

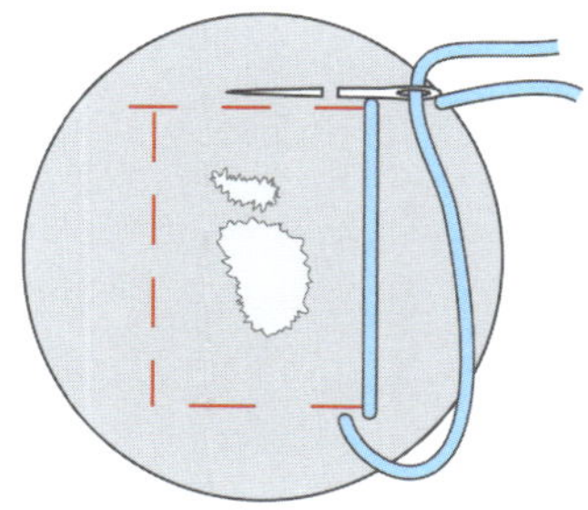

1 Place on the darning mushroom according to A on page 16. Using the blue thread, insert the needle at the top right, about 3cm (1¼in) outside the tacking (basting), and bring it out at the top right corner of the tacking.

2 Bring the needle down vertically and insert at the bottom right corner, bringing it out about 2mm (approx. 1/16in) to the left.

3 This time, take the needle up vertically, insert it one needle width away from the first warp thread and then bring it out 2mm (approx. 1/16in) to the left.

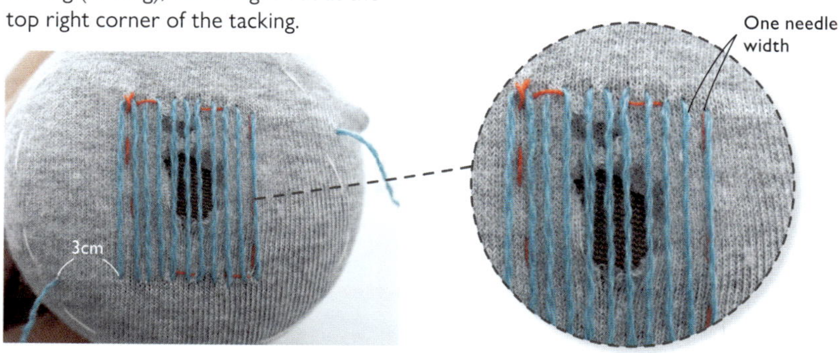

4 When you have finished the warp threads, take the needle out 3cm (1¼in) away. It does not matter if you end at the top or at the bottom.

Keep one needle width space

Unless you have some space between the warp threads, it is hard to pass the weft through. Make sure you leave one needle's width between warp threads.

Weft

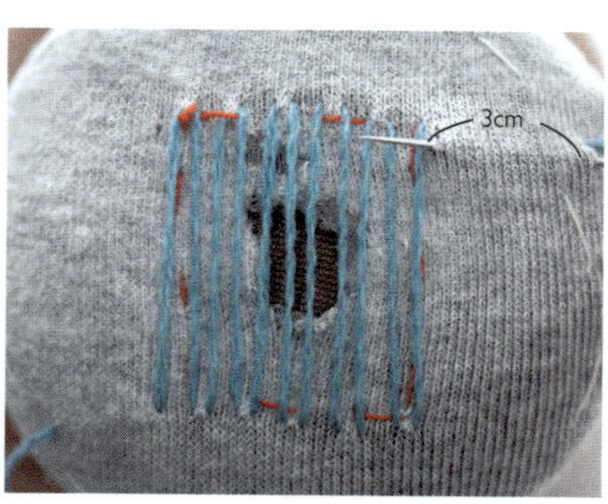

5 Thread the needle with yellow green thread, insert it 3cm (1¼in) outside the top right corner and bring it out at the right top corner.

6 Pass the needle over and under each alternating warp thread, picking up the sock and reinforcing material when passing underneath the warp.

7 When you have finished passing the weft through the warp, make one stitch.

THREADS USED:

Cashmere yarn
(blue, Yellow, Yellow green)

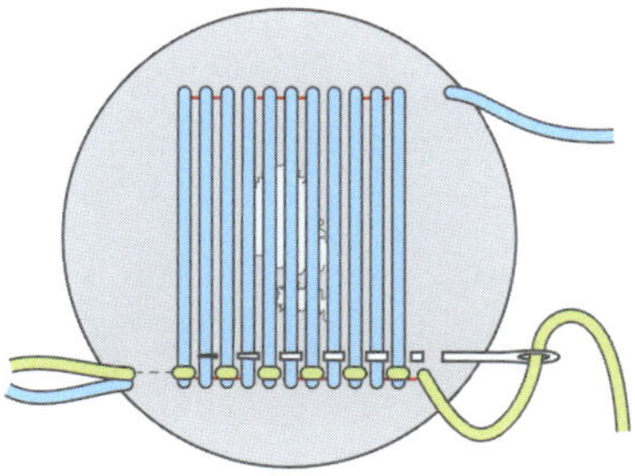

8 Turn the darning mushroom by 180 degrees and work in the alternate sequence to the previous row: if your first horizontal row passed over and then under the warp, the next should pass under and then over. At the end of the row, make a stitch.

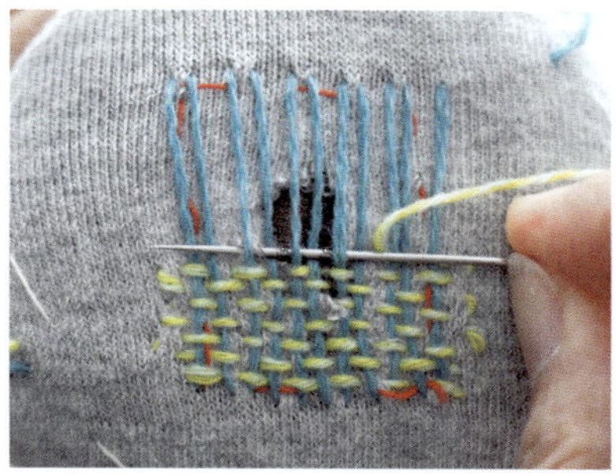

9 When you come to the hole, pick up the tights material with your needle. It is not essential to pick up the sock or tights material every time you pass the warp.

CHANGING THE THREAD

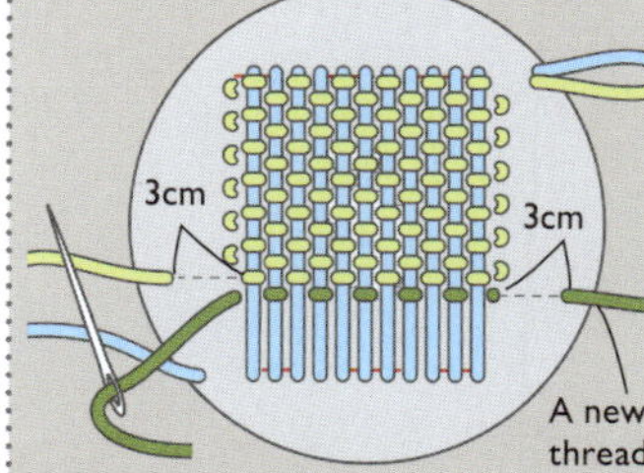

10 When you only have a small amount of thread left, bring the needle out 3cm (1¼in) outside the darning and take the thread out of the needle. Thread the needle with a new thread, insert it 3cm (1¼in) outside the darning and bring it out just before the warp.

Finishing Ends

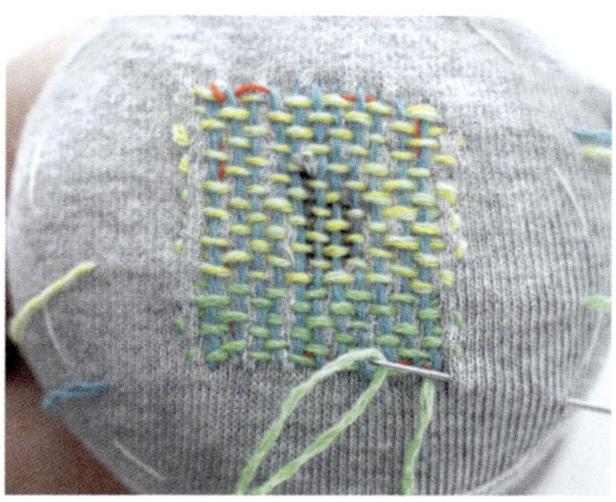

11 When you finish with the weft, insert the needle, bring it out 3cm (1¼in) outside the darning and take the thread out of the needle.

Turn to RS

12 Remove the tacking and the darning mushroom, turn WS out and cut the ends to 1cm (⅜in) to finish. If you don't like leaving the ends loose, pass the threads under some stitches. Trim the tights materials and you are done.

Finished

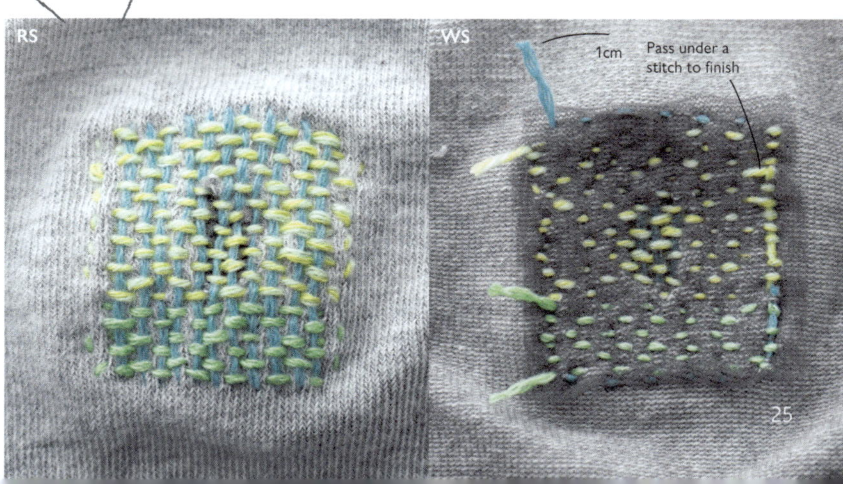

Cut to 1cm (⅜in). Pass under a stitch to finish.

Technique 5

Raised seed stitch

Decorative darning based on seed stitch.
Use cashmere and wool threads, try using several different yarns combined in the same needle.

THREADS USED:
Acrylic yarn (blue), cashmere wool (yellow green), wool silk thread (white/green)

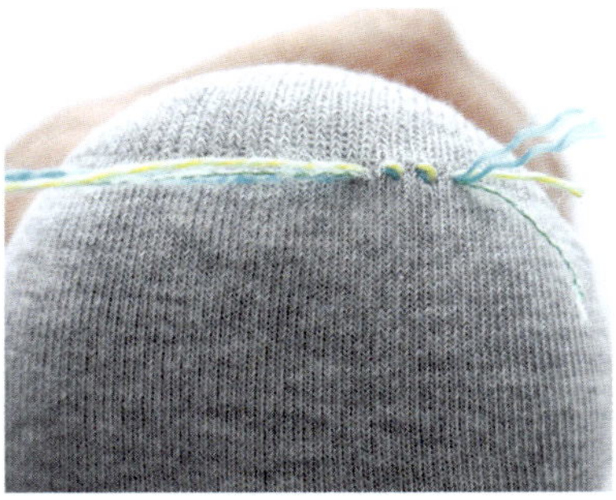

1 Work two seed stitches by stitching forwards 5mm (1/4in) and back 2mm (approx. 1/16in) twice.

2 The next time you go back 2mm (approx. 1/16in), do not pull the thread through – leave a loop.

3 Repeat step 2 to continue the row.

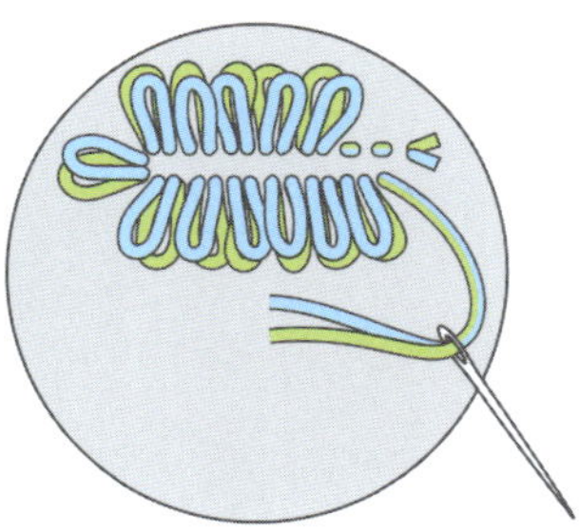

4 Stitch from right to left and turn at a convenient location to start another row.

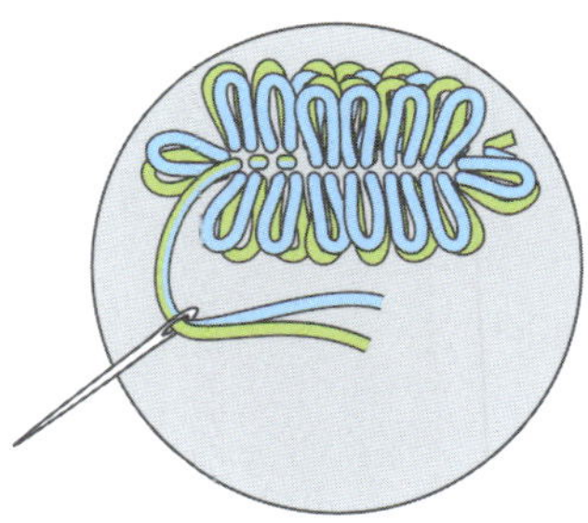

5 Now stitch in between the two rows.

6 To finish, work one seed stitch and cut the thread.

By inserting a knitting needle through the loops and gently pulling them, you can produce same size loops. If you cut the loops, they become like carpet or velvet.

Technique 6

Repairing the sock cuff

You cannot darn loosened openings, but don't give up. Fix it simply by using an elastic thread.

Shirring elastic is used for sleeve cuffs for commercially available sweaters. Use a blunt yarn needle or a tapestry needle with elastic thread.

A loose sock cuff makes the sock look baggy. When this happens, the sock no longer fits the leg well.

1 Insert the needle from the WS.

2 Pick up some stitches and pass the elastic thread through.

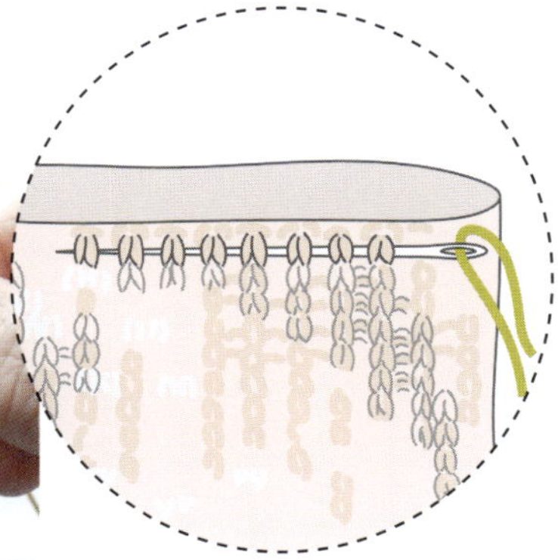

If you have socks with tight openings, you could take out the rubber thread and make them looser using the same procedure.

Go around three times.

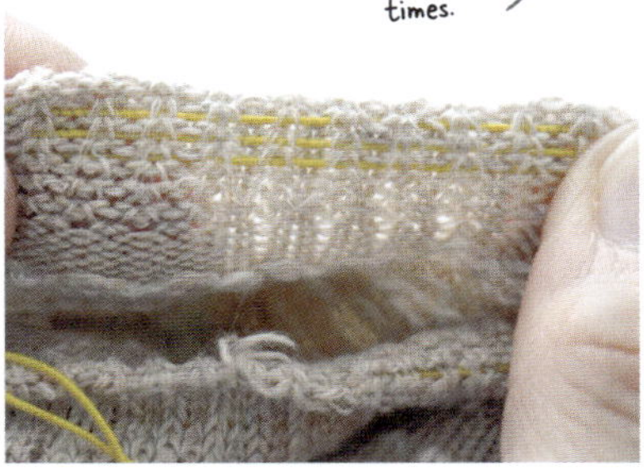

3 Continue to pass the thread through three rows. Once one row is done, put the sock on to adjust for the preferred size.

4 Once you have finished three rows, try it on one more time, adjust to the suitable size and double knot the end. Cut the ends.

Stitches used in this book

There are lots of other stitches that could be used for darning.
These are good not only for repairing, but also for decoration.

Running stitch

Recommended for light reinforcement. It is not recommended for a wide range of darning as it is not elastic.

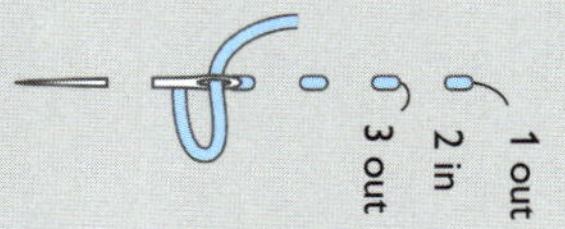

Tambourine stitch

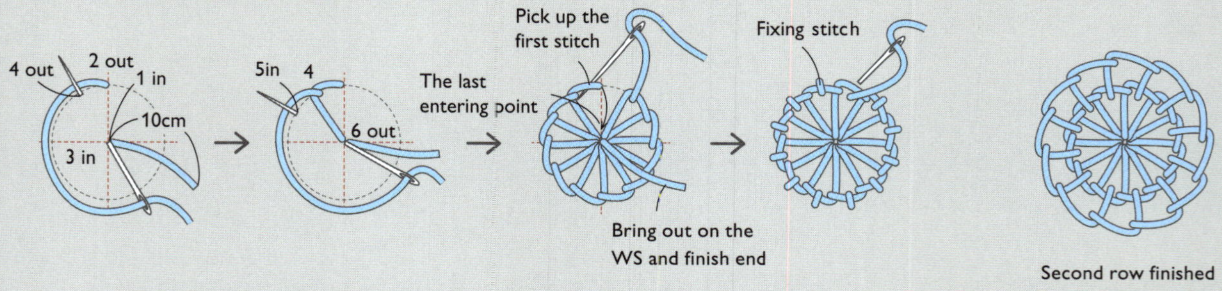

Y-stitch

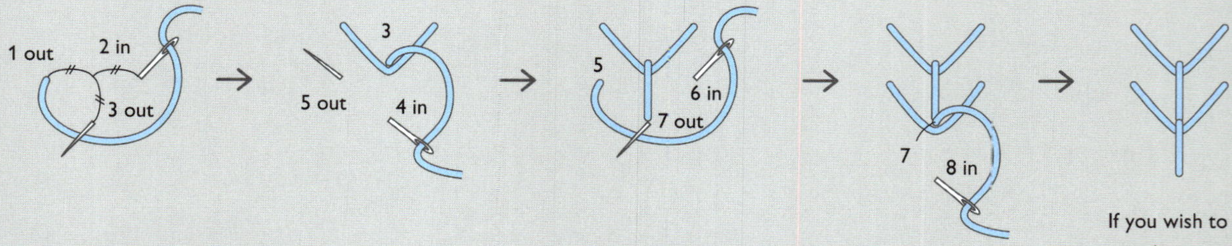

If you wish to continue, repeat steps 5–8

Zigzag parallel honeycomb stitch

A reversible technique with a zigzag pattern on the RS and a rain-like pattern on the WS. It is possible to apply it to circular honeycomb too.

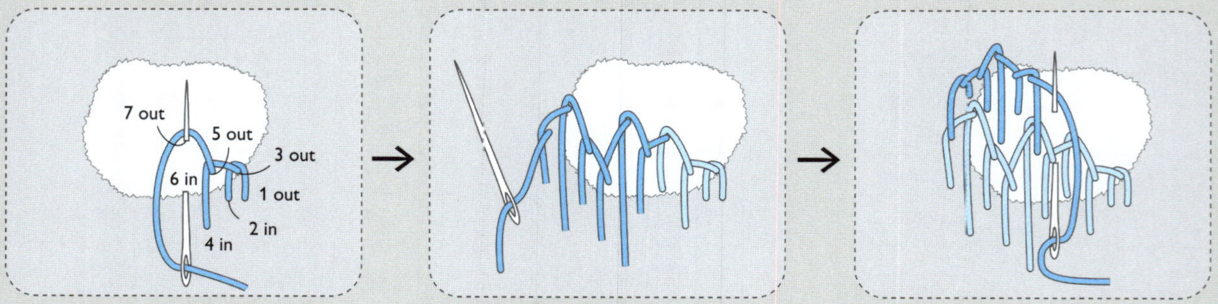

Feel free to vary the position of needle insertion or the stitch length.

Second row, it is not necessary to insert in positions below the first row.

◎ Swiss darning

A technique where a new thread is applied to flesh out an old yarn thinned by friction.

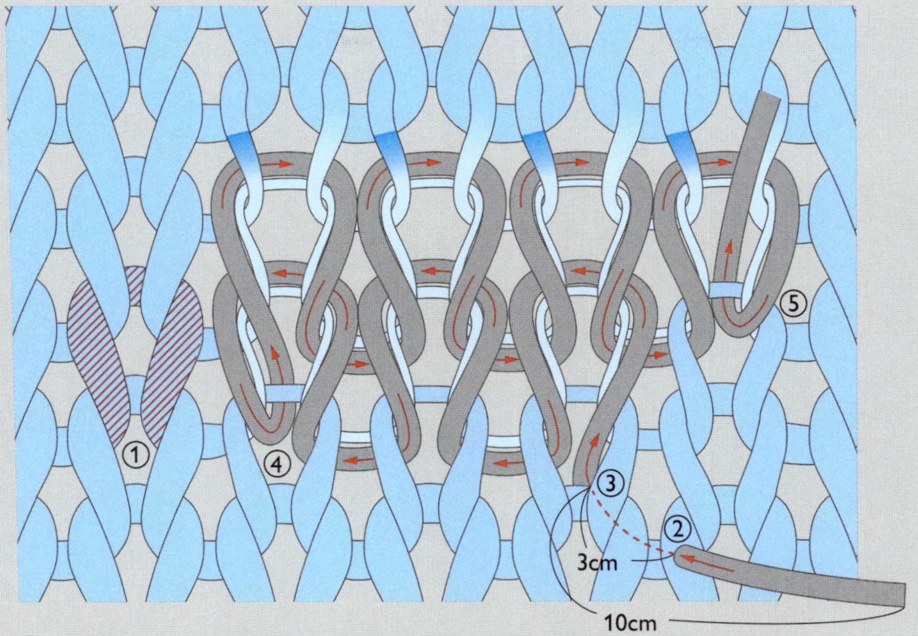

① Observe carefully so that your eyes become used to the shape of the stitches.

② Insert the needle 3cm (1¼in) outside of the worn area. Leave a 10cm (4in) thread tail and finish on the WS.

③ Bring the needle out at the arrow sign and pass the needle and thread through the fabric following the arrow signs.

④ Move up to the second row.

⑤ Move up to the third row.

Choosing techniques effectively

If you know which stitches work best for the kind of damage, you can be more effective when repairing.

△ Possible given a particular condition ○ Possible ◎ Recommended

		Running stitch p28	Seed stitch p22	English basket p24	Circular honeycomb p20	Parallel honeycomb p18
Thin		△ Two directions	○ Makes it last longer	○ Makes it last longer	◎ Makes it last much longer	◎ Makes it last much longer
Very thin	small area	△ Two directions	○ Two directions	◎	◎	◎
	large area	○ Patch: one sheet of tights	○ Patch: one sheet of tights	○ Patch: one sheet of tights	◎ Patch: one sheet of tights	◎ Patch: one sheet of tights
Small hole (nail of your little finger)		○ Need a patch	○ Need a patch	◎	◎ Patch: one sheet of tights	◎ Patch: one sheet of tights
Large hole and tights material		△ Possible but takes time (only for the flat area of the ball)	△ Possible but takes time	○ Patch: one sheet of tights	◎ Patch: two sheets of tights	◎ Patch: two sheets of tights

Thin socks

Fine socks for spring and summer are easily damaged and tend to develop holes in no time. As most of these socks are made with synthetic yarns such as nylon or polyester, it is best to apply the same stocking material for darning to maintain the thinness.

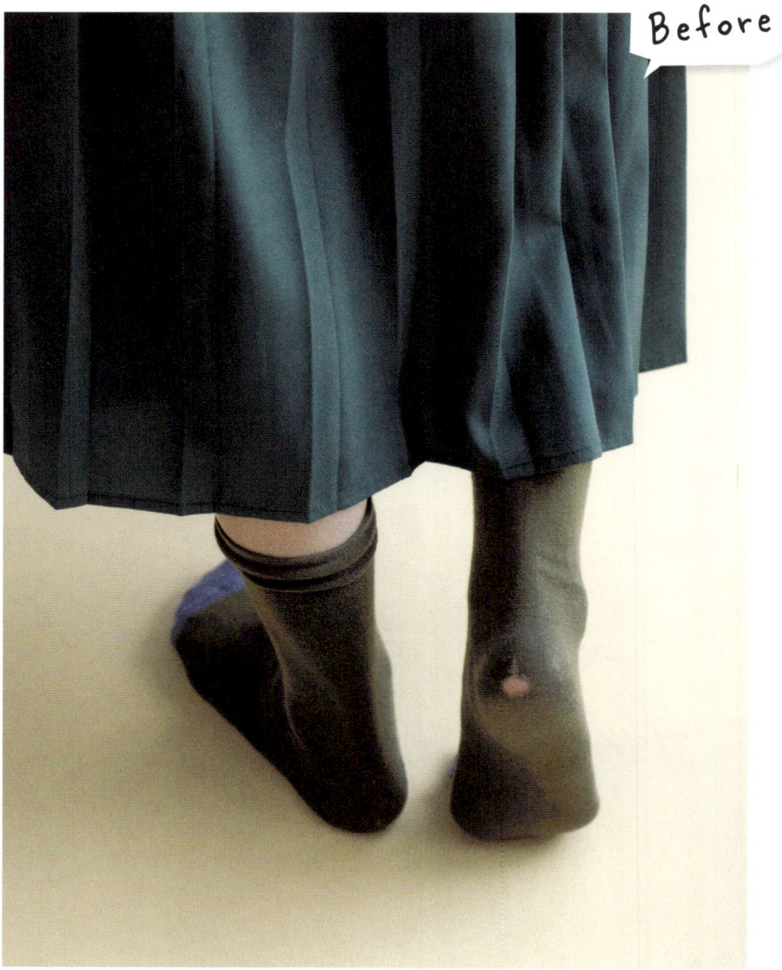

Case 1

The area around the ball, below the big toe, becomes thin. A hole develops in the heel and serious fraying starts.

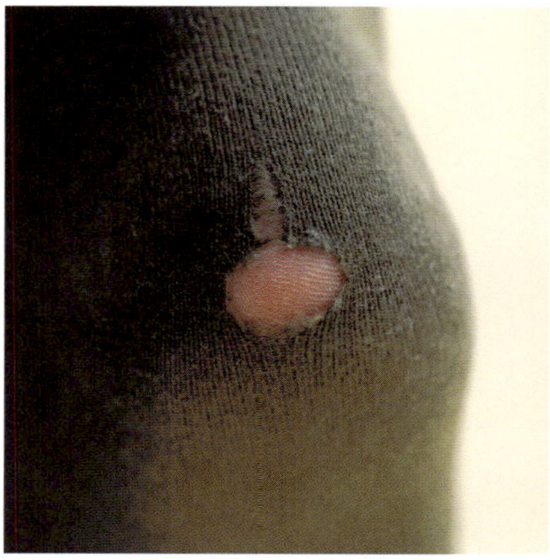

Technique and thread used

a. Apply the tights material (see page 16), work circular honeycomb stitch (see page 20) from the WS using silver glitter thread. Work tambourine stitches (see page 28) on top of that with orange cashmere yarn.

b. Work circular honeycomb stitch from the WS using silver glitter thread.

c. Tambourine stitches worked from the front with orange cashmere yarn and fluorescent yellow woolly yarn.

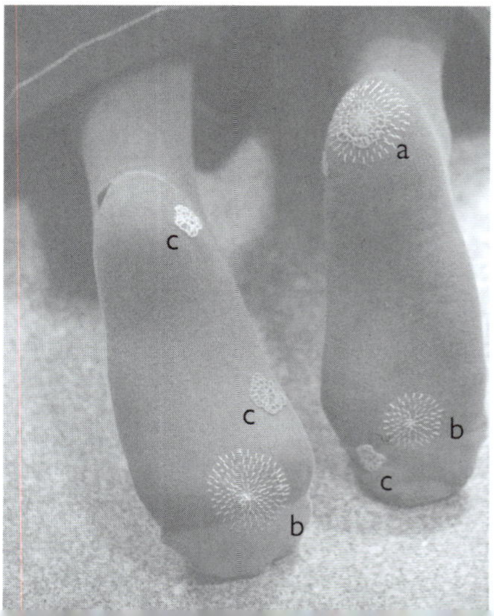

The sole of socks that children would love!

This was a special request from the owner of the socks, who looks after children for work, to make stiches on the sole of the sock in colours and patterns that are appealing to children. Priority was given to repairing the damaged area, and tambourine stitches were also used for decorative purposes.

For the heel, apply tights material. For damage around the ball of the foot, glitter nylon thread was used to work circular honeycomb stitch from the WS.
From the RS, the stitches look like pretty fireworks.

Part 1

Thin socks

Before

Case 2

There is a hole at the tip of the big toe, and both the front and the back of the toe area has degenerated and thinned.

Technique and thread used

a. Tights patch applied to the hole (see page 16) and darned with circular honeycomb stitch from the WS (see page 20). For the thinned area, small, round honeycomb stitches were added from both the WS and RS.

b. Circular honeycomb stitches worked from both the WS and RS.

c. In between, tipsy stitches added here and there randomly.*

All the threads used are woolly thread.

First close off the hole, and then apply honeycomb stitches – working from both the WS and RS – to the whole of the toe area. Stitch over a 2cm (¾in) diameter area, like the area of the hole and fill in the space between with tipsy stitches to strengthen.

*Tipsy stitches are those in which every stitch faces a different direction.

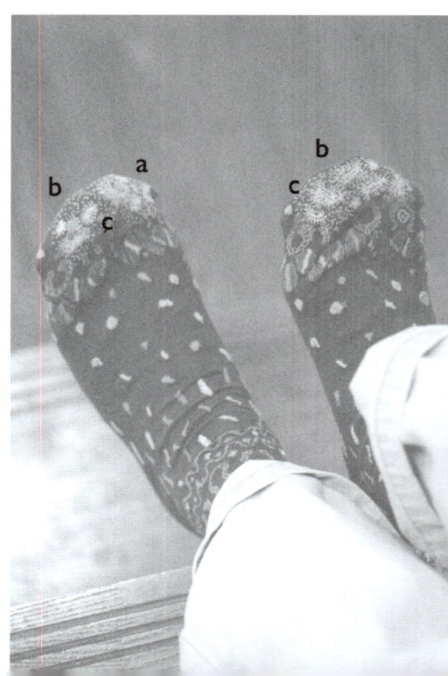

After

Use the colours in the sock

If you have beautiful patterned or coloured socks, then it is good to darn with that design in mind. By selecting similar colours, your mending will blend in. You can also use the shapes used in the sock pattern for inspiration when darning.

Woolly thread is thin and strong and is perfect for darning thin socks.

Thin socks

Case 3

Heavily thinned toe tips. Here, no additional material was added, but dense tambourine stitches were worked from the WS of the fabric, and the same thread was used to create decorative flowers on the top of the foot and around the ankle.

Technique and thread used

a. Tambourine stitch (see page 28) from the WS). For the thinned area, small, round honeycomb stitches were added from both the WS and RS.

b. Ankle: Y-stitches (see page 28) towards the centre of the circle, repeated radially. All worked with woolly thread.

Case 4

Soft mohair or woolly thread was chosen to match the colours and the decoration on the socks. The thinned heel area has been darned with 1–2cm (3⁄8in–3⁄4in) of round honeycomb stitch and tambourine stiches to fill.

Technique and thread used

1–2cm (3⁄8in–3⁄4in) of circular honeycomb stitches (see page 20) were added in several different places, both from the WS and RS, then tambourine stitches were added (see page 28). Lemon and light khaki mohair yarn. Gold and wisteria purple woolly thread. Coral pink No. 25 embroidery thread.

Case 5

Woolly thread with glitter has been used that matches the glittery and gorgeous pattern on these socks. The darning is added like a mosaic so that more can be added as and when the damage expands.

Technique and thread used

a. For the heavily thinned area, tights material was applied (see page 16). Parallel honeycomb stitch (see page 18) worked in triangles or rectangles from the WS.

b. No patch material was used for the thinned area, parallel honeycomb was added from the RS and the WS. All the threads used are woolly threads.

Case 6

These knit socks with a Hawaiian pattern were heavily damaged around the ball of the foot. The damaged area was darned with wavy honeycomb stitches made with boucle mohair yarn.

Technique and thread used

a. Raised seed stitch (see page 26) with thick boucle mohair yarn.

b. A nylon mesh patch attached from the RS with seed stitches (see page 22) using nylon thread.

Part 2

Everyday socks

Normal thickness socks can be worn in all seasons and come in a wide range of materials. Natural fibres such as cotton, wool, linen and silk are often mixed with synthetic fibres and can become thinned and worn through friction.

Before

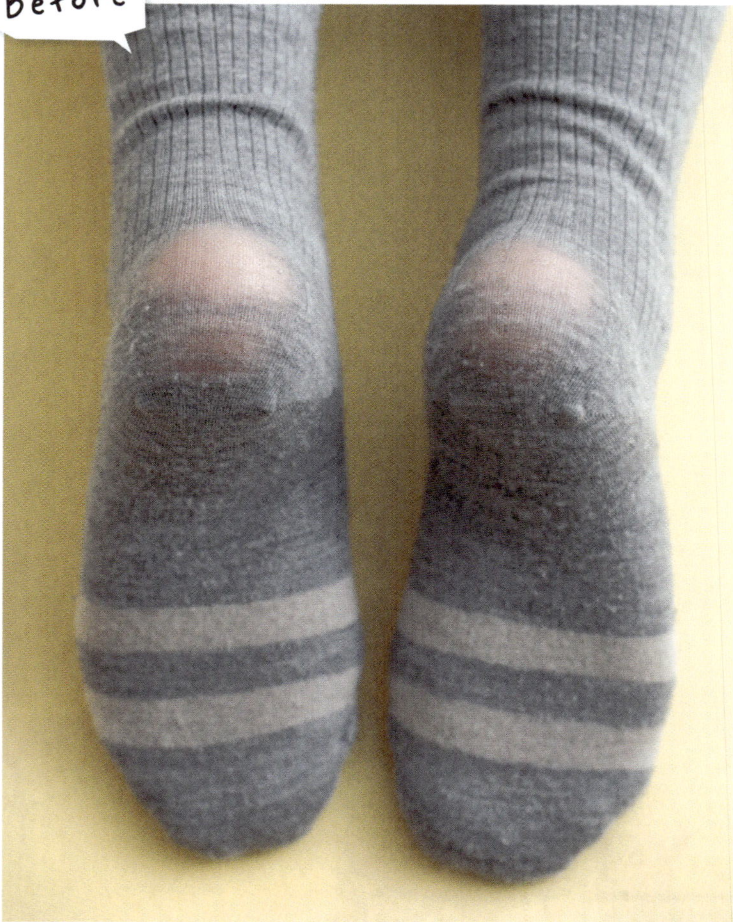

Case 7

Smart adult long socks made from good quality extra-fine wool mix yarn in light grey with wide stripes. The backs of the heels had become splendidly worn out.

Technique and thread used

Circular honeycomb stitch (see page 20), worked from the RS using wool/silk thread.

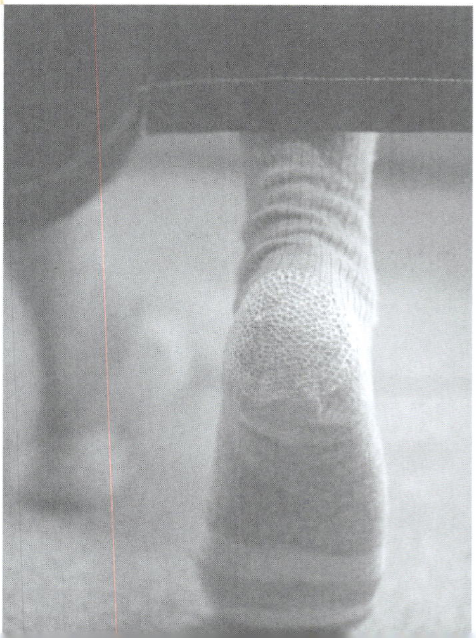

Stitch densely to strengthen

When a sock is so severely damaged, it can be tempting to use a tights patch, but in this case, round honeycomb stitches have been applied over a wide area using extra-fine wool/silk mix thread. Make sure not to pull too hard when stitching to avoid the darned area becoming hard or lumpy.

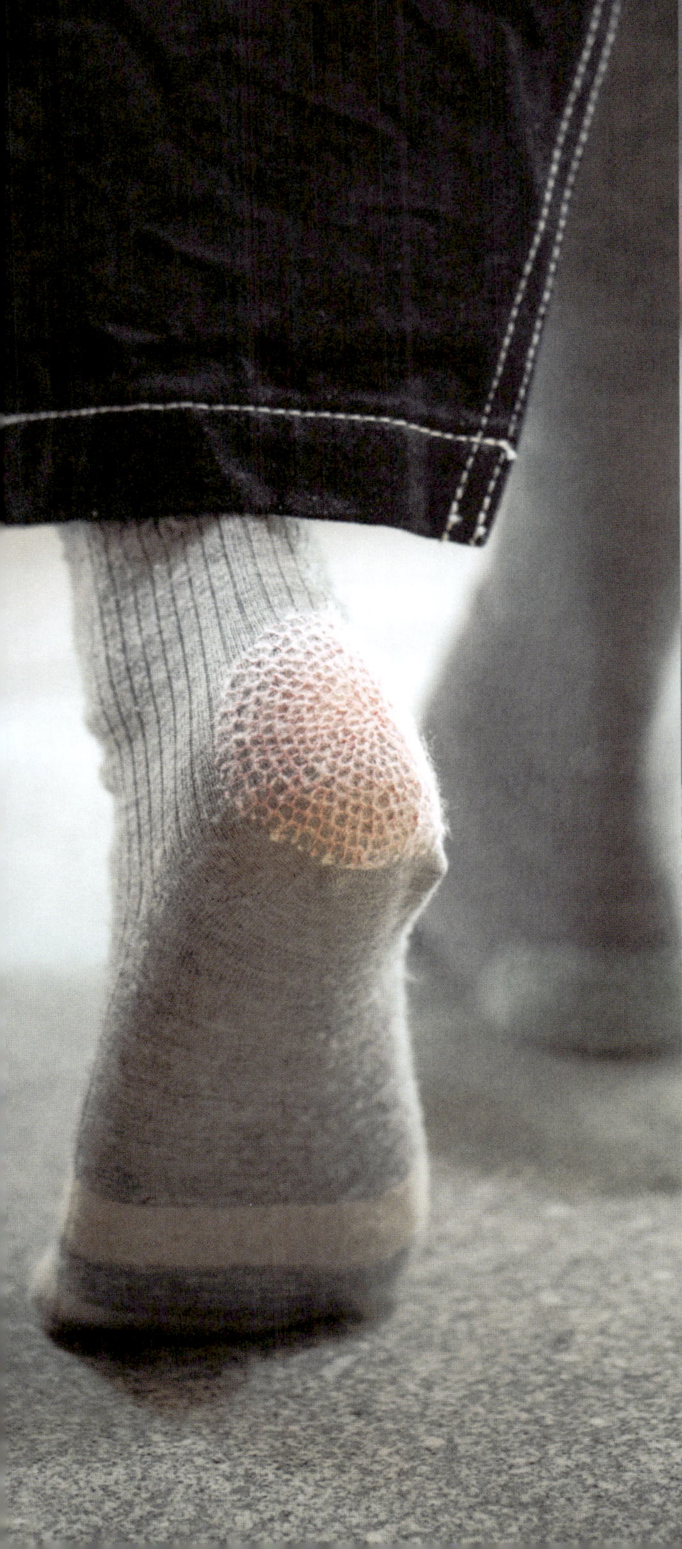

Honeycomb stitches look beautiful, even from the WS, and are brilliantly comfortable to wear.

Part 2

Everyday socks

Before

Technique and thread used

a. Tights material patch applied to the hole (see page 16) and round honeycomb stitch worked from the RS (see page 20) using cashmere yarn.

b. Parallel honeycomb stitch from the RS and WS (see page 18), worked with cashmere yarn.

c. Fan-shaped tambourine stiches (see page 28), worked from the RS with yellow and blue cashmere yarn and chunky yellow boucle mohair yarn. Turned WS out to apply a patch of black tights material and work round honeycomb stitch from the WS.
The tips of the toes were also reinforced with parallel honeycomb stitches in various directions and shapes. Decorative darning on the ankles and calves.

Case 8

A hole with a diameter of 2cm (¾in) has appeared in the tip of the big toe. Many colours are woven into the flowers on these beautiful socks, making you think, 'it would be a shame to throw them away!'

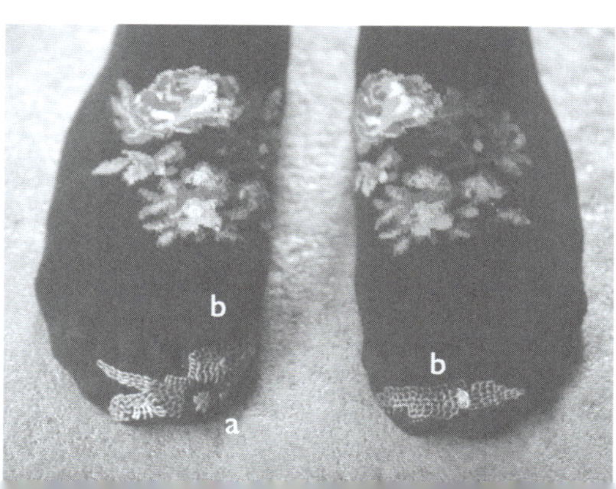

Making good use of a floral pattern

Cashmere and mohair yarns in colours matched to those used in the socks pattern have been used to preserve the look of these gorgeous socks. The hole in the big toe was filled with a patch of black tights material and covered with circular honeycomb stitch with black thread. Pink thread was used for the centre to make a point.

Make decorative tambourine stitches that look like butterfly wings.

Replicate the feel of the floral pattern using parallel honeycomb stitches in different shapes, using different colour threads.

Part 2

Everyday socks

Case 9

The damage is concentrated in the heels, but this time, tights patches were not used, instead the damage was darned with durable sock yarn and extra-fine boucle mohair yarn.

Technique and thread used

a. Parallel honeycomb (see page 18) was worked from the RS in rectangles or triangles using sock yarn.

b. Parallel honeycomb, worked from the RS in triangle shapes as decoration, worked with extra-fine boucle mohair yarn

Case 10

Tabi socks with moderate thinning damage on the back of the heel and the tip of the big toe.

Technique and thread used

a. Rectangles of parallel honeycomb (see page 18) – stitched vertically and horizontally – worked from the RS and applied to an area larger than the damage.

b. Circular honeycomb, worked from the RS (see page 20) – all the threads used are split from sock yarn.

Case 11

Soft, fluffy, patterned knit socks. The base and outside of the heel and the ball of the foot were heavily worn out.

Technique and thread used

a. Tights material patch applied (see page 16) and parallel honeycomb stitch (see page 18) worked from the WS.

b. Tights material patch applied and circular honeycomb stitch (see page 20) worked from the WS.

c. Tights material patch applied and parallel honeycomb applied from the RS – all threads are extra-fine boucle mohair yarn.

Case 12

These red, glittery tabi socks were patched with material from a polka dot tulle sock. A glimpse of the pattern in between stitches looks cute.

Technique and thread used

a. Tulle sock patch applied from the RS, and round honeycomb (see page 20) worked from the RS – silver/glitter yarn and chunky white boucle mohair yarn.

b. Parallel honeycomb (see page 18) and seed stitch worked from the WS, (see page 22) – silver/glitter yarn and chunky white boucle mohair yarn.

Warm socks

Even when they are worn out, it's hard to throw away warm socks made of high-quality yarn such as wool, alpaca or cashmere. Darning means you can keep using them for a while longer and selecting the correct yarn will help with balancing durability with texture and warmth.

Before

Case 13

Thick and fluffy socks made from highest grade Mongolian wool, even just touching it makes you feel warm! The wool fibres have been worn through friction, and the outside of the heel has become thinned down to the synthetic threads.

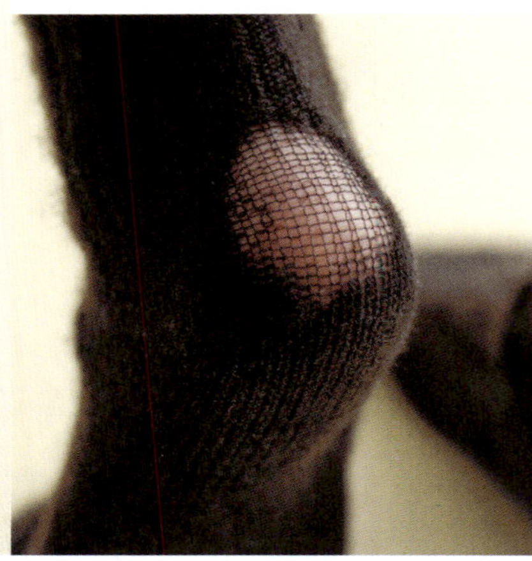

Technique and thread used

Tights material patch applied (see page16) and triangular English basket (see page 24) worked from the RS. Hold one cashmere and one wool yarn together.

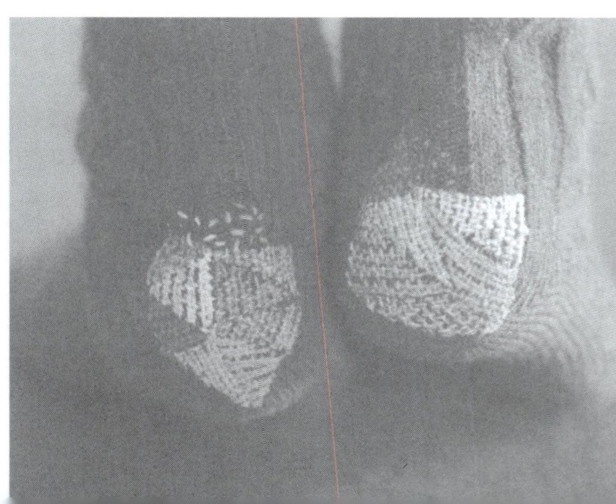

The colourful triangles look artistic

Triangular English basket stitch can be started at the centre, and then expanded by connecting the three sides for a well-balanced finish. If you continue stitching in neighbouring areas, your darning will become even more durable. If you have some thread left, make seed stitches in the surrounding areas.

Use bright colours to expand triangles from the centre to the outside.

WS

As your stitches scoop up small amounts of the patch material, you see small stitches on the WS.

Part 3

Warm socks

Case 14

Warm socks tend to prioritize warmth over appearance, so cool design is rare, but one look was all it took for me to fall in love with the delicate colour combination on these socks. Then I noticed there were big holes in the base of the heels.

Technique and thread used

A tights material patch (see page 16) and English basket stitch (see page 24) applied from the RS. The surrounding area was reinforced with seed stitches (see page 22). Yellow and green thread split from sock yarn and orange recycled sock yarn.

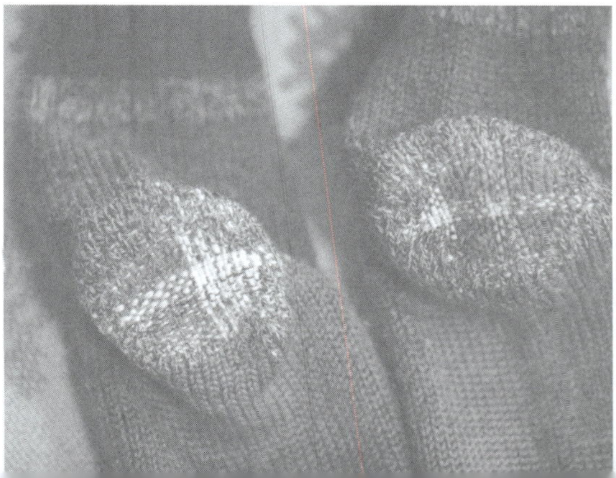

Strengthen big holes using patches

For big, gaping holes, use tights material patches to provide durability, and darn with English basket stitch. By using several different colours for warp and weft, a lattice pattern emerged. The surrounding area is strengthened even more with seed stitches.

WS A black tights patch was used for patching from the WS. Trimming the extra edges makes them comfortable to wear.

Warm socks

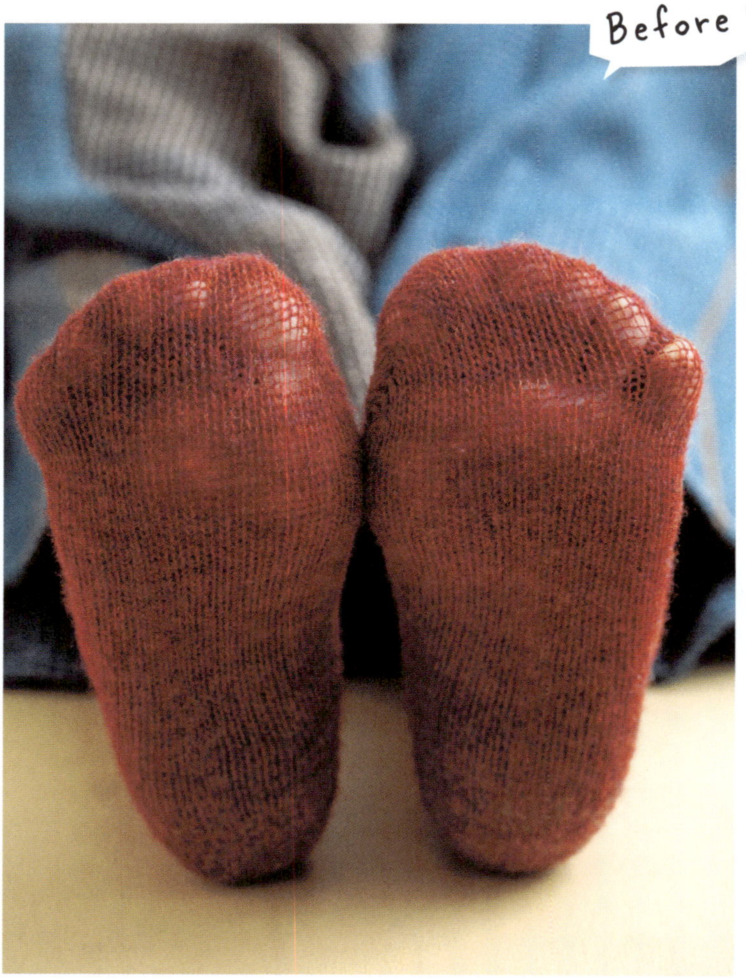

Case 15

From the tip of the toes to the heel, a wide area of these socks is worn out.

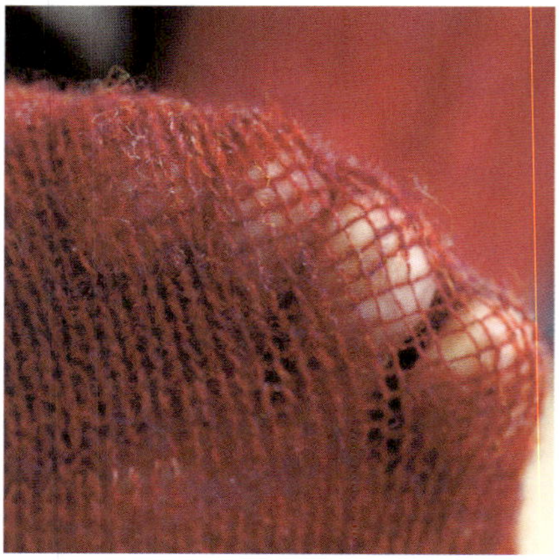

Technique and thread used

Working from the RS, parallel honeycomb stitch was worked on the thinned area (see page 18) and seed stitches (see page 22) on the surrounding area. Extra-fine boucle mohair yarn.

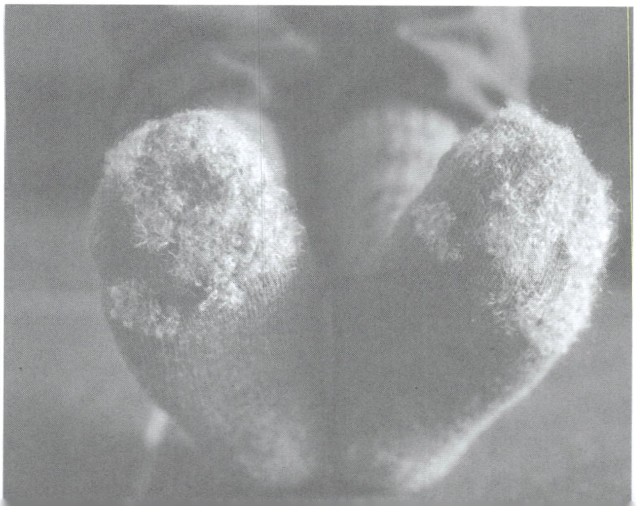

After

Fluffy boucle mohair yarn!

When the yarn of a thick sock has become thin, fluff it up with heat-retentive, elastic and durable boucle mohair yarn. Over time and use, loops become loosened and fluffy. As this is a large area, divide it into several 3cm (1¼in) ovals to stitch. The surrounding area can be reinforced with seed stitching for durable darning.

WS The WS of the tip of the toe where parallel honeycomb was applied.

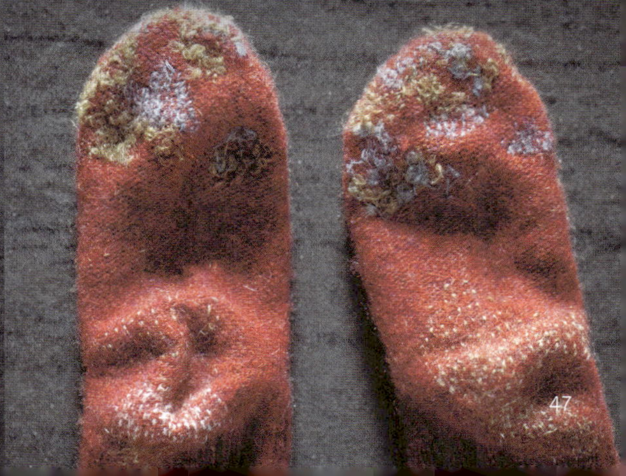

Warm socks

Case 16

The brushed wool around the heel and the ball of the foot look sadly worn out.

Technique and thread used

Seed stitch applied from the RS (see page 22) both vertically and horizontally – extra-thick boucle yarn.

Case 17

Firmly felted thick wool socks. The outside of the heel and the ball of the foot are both heavily worn.

Technique and thread used

a. From the RS, English basket stitch (see page 24).
b. From the RS, circular honeycomb (see page 20).
c. From the RS, zigzag circular honeycomb (see page 27).

All the threads are recycled sock yarn.

Case 18

Y-stitches that echo the Nordic pattern, with moss-like or branch-like organic shapes, were applied to the outside of the thinned heel, so that they are just visible even when wearing shoes.

Technique and thread used

a. Y-stitch (see page 28).

b. From the RS, parallel honeycomb (see page 18).

All threads are extra-thick boucle mohair yarns

Case 19

The damaged areas were repaired with round and parallel honeycomb stitches and scattered raised seed stitches to give depth to the pattern.

Technique and thread used

a. Raised seed (p26) – extra-fine wool yarn.

b. Tights material patch applied to the hole (see page 16) and circular honeycomb (see page 20) worked from the WS. For the heavily thinned area, a tights patch was added and parallel honeycomb (see page 18) worked from the WS – medium-thin sock yarn.

Work socks

Socks designed to match suits or uniforms prioritize utility over fashion. In these cases, it's best to make repairs less noticeable. Keep matching or similar colour threads to hand so that you can darn at any time.

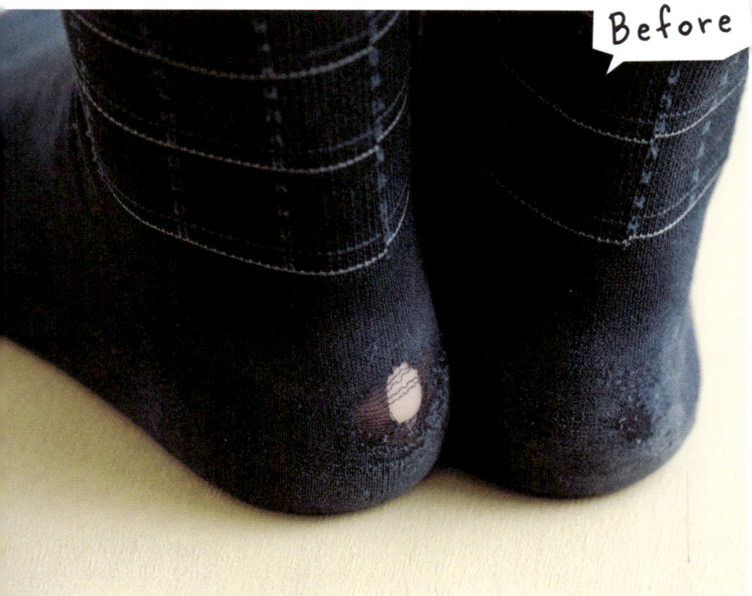

Case 20

Commuting socks to match suits. A small hole had appeared on the heel of the left sock and the right heel was moderately worn.

Technique and thread used

For the hole on the left heel, a tights material patch was applied (see page 16), and on top of the hole, and in the surrounding area, three 2cm (¾in) areas of rectangular seed stitch (see page 22) were worked at various angles.

Thinning on the right heel – about three 2cm (¾in) areas of rectangular seed stitch at contrasting angles. All threads are wool yarn.

Establish both durability and comfort

To ensure durability, the thicker briefs section of the tights was used for patching. Also, woolly threads, which are high in elasticity and flexibility. To ensure comfort, avoid darning too densely.

Case 21

The owner of these socks has several pairs of brown patterned socks to match their company uniform. For the thinned area, the request was to make sure the look of the darning fitted the rest of the socks.

To ensure that the finish would match the socks, most threads selected were in colours very close to the ones in the socks. Recycled sock yarn was used to ensure durability

Honeycomb stitched from the WS meant the RS showed patterns resembling fireworks.

The WS, where round honeycomb stitch was applied.

Technique and thread used

From the WS, circular honeycomb (see page 20). Mixed colour space-dyed recycled sock yarn.

Socks with ladders

Sports socks, particularly football socks, are prone to ladders. This is a phenomenon whereby a hole leads to dropped stitches. By using a tool called a latch hook, and repairing with a thread of a similar colour, you can repair a ladder to a level where you can hardly see it.

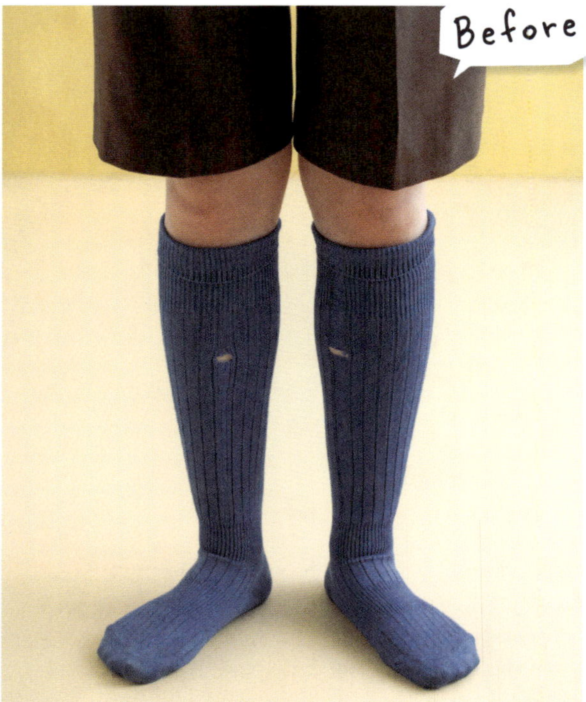

Case 22

The purpose of sports socks is to protect the legs, and as most of them are densely knit using synthetic threads, once there is a hole, it can easily lead to dropped stitches and ladders.

Reknit the dropped stitches.

Use the latch hook to re-knit the dropped stitches. It is detailed work, but once you are used to it, it is not difficult. The final remaining hole can be closed off easily with English basket stitch (see page 24) using woolly thread.

How to mend ladders

1 Find the dropped stitch at the bottom of the ladder.

2 Catch the stitch using the latch hook.

3 Insert the latch hook beneath the next rung of yarn above and the lever on the latch hook will open up.

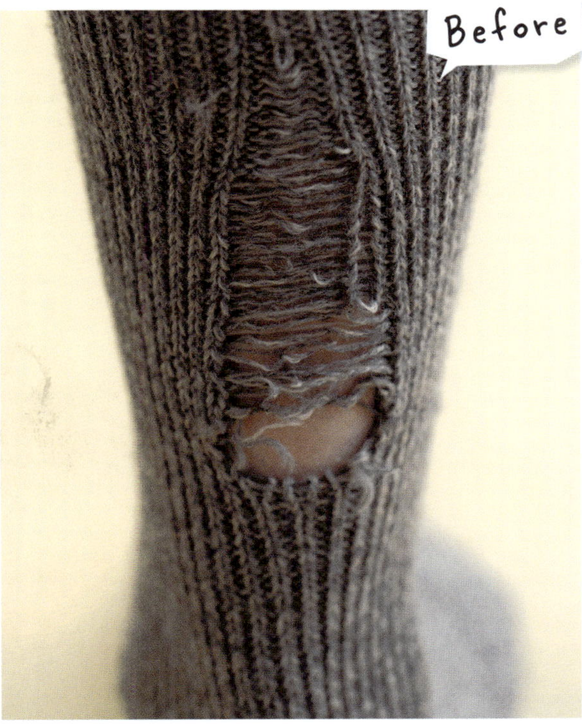

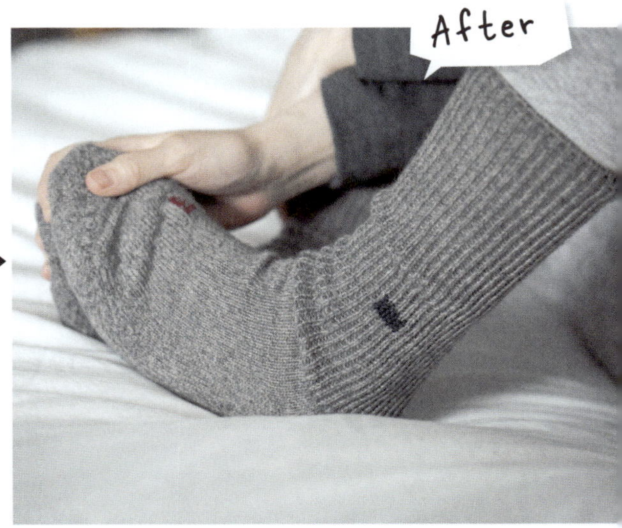

Even the large hole becomes smaller!

Even such a serious ladder can be fixed using a latch hook, picking up stitches one by one, leading to a much smaller hole. The small hole can then be filled using English basket stitch (see page 24) using wool thread, which becomes an accent.

Case 23

Thick wool socks for wearing with high boots. The zip of the boot caught the sock, rapidly leading to the emergence of a ladder and a massive hole.

What is a latch hook?

It is a tool with a hook with a small lever that opens and closes. You can use a crochet hook if you don't have a latch hook.

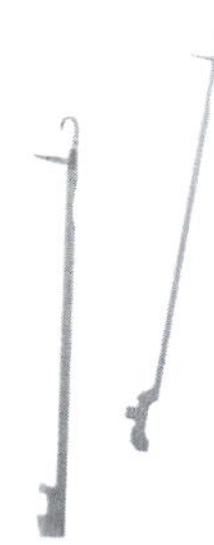

4 Pull the latch hook towards you and the lever will close.

3 The original stitch will fall off the hook and one stitch has been restored. Repeat as many times as needed to restore all the stitches in the ladder.

Part 6

Sport socks

Sport socks are made based on scientific research about muscle movement, avoiding fatigue, and durability. They tend to be expensive as they are specialized. It's wise to keep checking how comfortable they feel as you darn, stitching a little at a time.

Case 24

Running socks bought for running a full marathon. There is a hole by the big toenail.

Technique and thread used

Darning stick used to apply a patch of tights material (see page 17) and English basket stitch (see page 24) worked with wool thread on the RS of the socks.

Prioritizing comfort in repair

To achieve comfort, it is best to avoid threads or stitches that result in an uneven surface. These socks are not elastic, so the big toe holes were patched from the WS and English basket stitch applied from the RS.

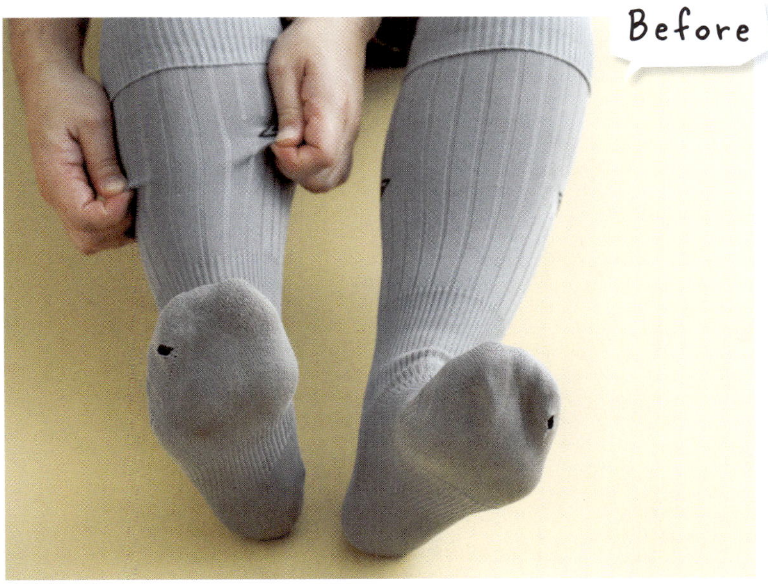

Case 25

Football socks repaired in preparation for a match. The habit of putting weight on one side of the foot led to holes by the little toes, and toe tips and heels became worn out.

Technique and threads used

a. A tights patch applied from the RS for the holes and English basket (see page 24) worked from the RS.
b. English basket from the RS.
c. Circular honeycomb (see page 20) from the RS.

All the threads are wool yarn.

To avoid discomfort on the sole, the patch is applied on the RS, so the inside of the sock is flat.

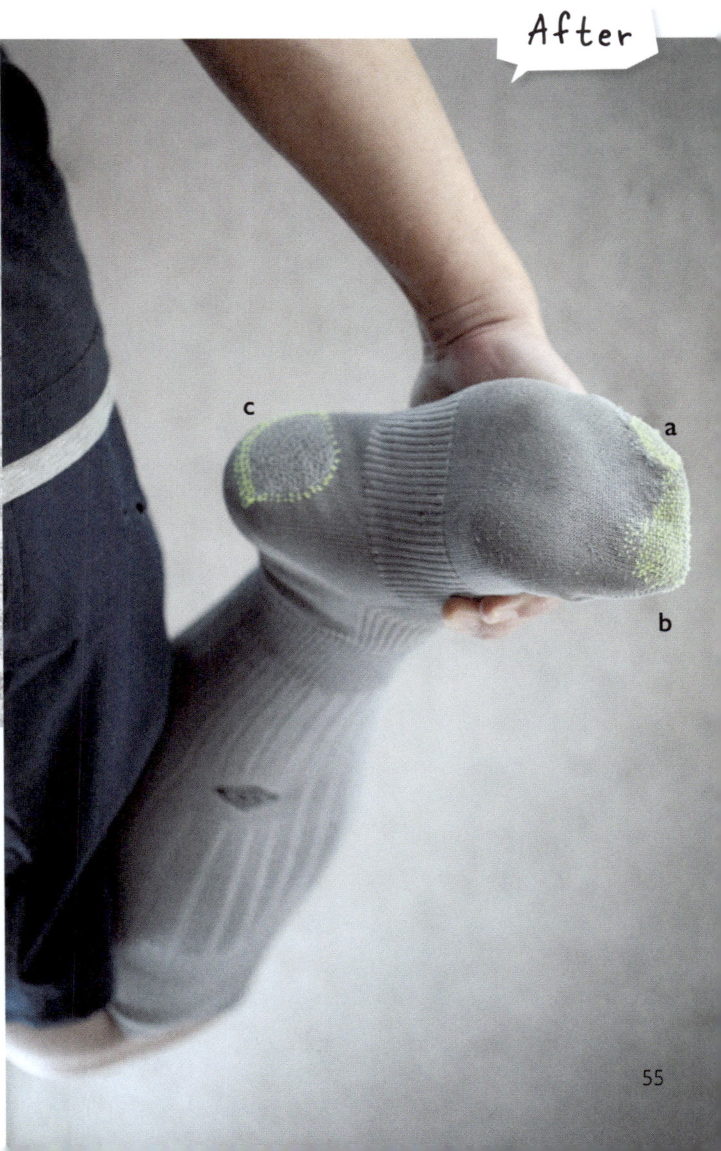

Applying the patch from the RS to prioritize comfort

To avoid the patch touching the foot, it was applied from the RS. English basket stitch was used for the toe tips, which are not elastic, and round honeycomb was used for the heels to focus on functionality.

Sport socks

Case 26

The owner of these socks is a snowboarding fan. By the time they noticed the pilling, the socks were already heavily thinned. Obvious pilling was removed with a pair of scissors, and boucle mohair yarn was used for the repair, selected for its elasticity and insulating properties.

Technique and threads used

Tights material patch applied (see page 16) and, from the RS, 2–3cm (¾–1¼in) squares of parallel honeycomb (see page 18) worked at different angles. Boucle mohair yarn.

Case 27

Dad's favourite pair of sports socks were wearing out at the heels and the balls of the foot. English basket stitch was applied with colourful step-dyed wool yarn. Wool yarn can shrink slowly to fit the foot shape with repeated wash and may provide the same effect as an insole.

Technique and threads used

From the RS, English basket stitch (see page 24) with woolly yarn and No. 25 embroidery threads combined.

Column 1

Sport socks and darning Art

British artist Celia Pym uses darning as an art form. In 'First one's the best', one of her major works, she displays a series of colourful sports socks decorated with diverse darning designs. The idea for the piece came from a workshop she organized for residents in redevelopment districts of the 2012 London Olympics. The participants learned how to darn using colourful yarn on brand new sports socks, which had been rejected for shipping as they were seconds. The workshop ended with the participants joking, 'If we become good enough, we might get darning orders from professional athletes!'

During the workshop, Celia noticed that the brand new, machine-knitted sports socks went through a transformation once darning was applied – to such an extent that the normal adjectives, such as 'dynamic' or 'sporty', were no longer appropriate.

For 'First one's the best', she cut, punched, and applied darning to 60 pairs of sports socks using every bit of space on the socks. Brand new sports socks were butchered, but there was a beguiling beauty and strength in them – they all 'recovered' from being full of injuries. They were like Olympic athletes. Their perfect body and performance rested on their unimaginable physical and psychological challenges and conflicts. Invisible to the rest of the world, they diligently worked past issues and through such effort, they reached performance level. Celia's quiet and patient darning work on new socks led her to discover an artistic meaning, and led her to sublimate it into art. If you focus on darning seriously, you might one day reach such a realm.

Later, Celia conducted an experimental workshop in collaboration with a professor of medicine from King's College, London. Placing her mending desk in the corner of the Dissecting Room at the college, Pym darned and darned – repairing clothes brought in by students and staff. The students around Celia, exhausted from their lab work, found Celia's work healing.

Celia Pym

Born in 1978. English artist. Read sculpture at Harvard University and textile art at the Royal College of Art. Encountered darning through knitting, developed her theme of 'things and humans' and works in London. She teaches at the Royal College of Art, but also offers classes in craft shops to spread the art of darning. Her book *On Mending: Stories of damage and repair* is published by Quickthorn. Celiapym.com @celiapym

Slipper socks

These are worn only at home, so one tends to ignore the wear and tear and continue to wear them. They usually end up with holes in the heel, so the key is to repair them with threads and patches that provide cushioning and elasticity for comfort.

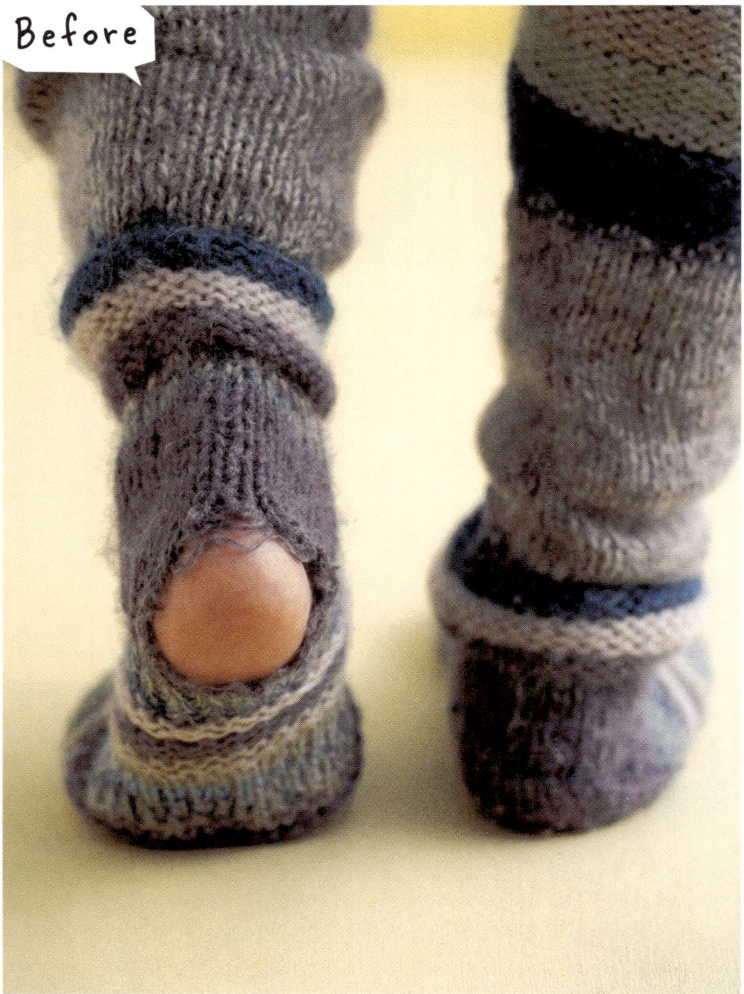

Case 28

Long slipper socks, the owner's favourites as they suffer from cold shins. They had intended to darn when there was only light damage, but by the time they noticed, the whole heel area was one gigantic hole. The base had also eroded a lot over the years.

Technique and threads used

a. Parallel honeycomb worked from the WS (see page 18) using extra-fine boucle mohair yarn.

b. Tights patch applied (see page 16) and seed stitch (see page 22) worked from the RS with extra fine boucle mohair yarn.

c. Tights patch applied; round honeycomb (see page 20) worked from the RS with extra-thick boucle mohair yarn.

d. For the centre of the damaged area, tambourine stitches (see page 28) worked with extra-thick boucle mohair yarn.

e. Circular honeycomb worked around the tambourine stitches using extra-fine boucle mohair yarn.

f. Y-stitches (see page 28) were used for ladders, stitched with extra thick boucle mohair yarn.

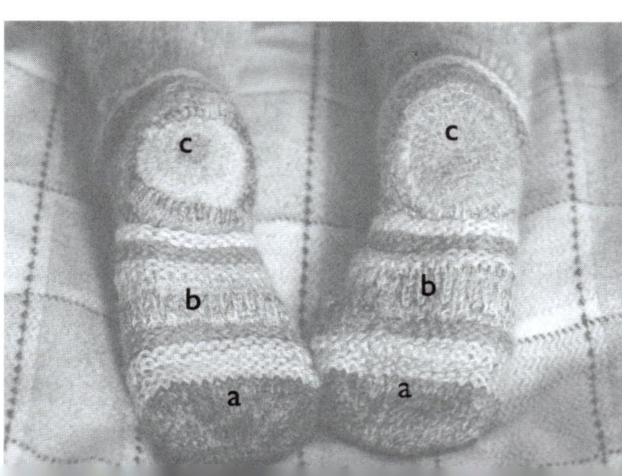

Close up the hole and strengthen further

To make the repair durable, the patch was applied to the gaping hole at the heel from the WS, and repaired with darning from the RS. Mohair yarn was selected for rough stitches for durability, elasticity and insulation.

The soles were strengthened with patches made from tights material.

Y-stitches were used to mend the ladder on the side of the sock, plus flower-like tambourine stiches.

Part 7

Slipper socks

Before

Case 29

Mohair hiking socks that have been cherished for nearly a decade. They were covered with pilling, the bottoms had lost the mohair texture though rubbing and they no longer offered anything close to warm comfort. This is a deterioration of socks that deserves attention as a darning case.

Technique and threads used

Parallel honeycomb (see page 28) worked from the WS using British wool.

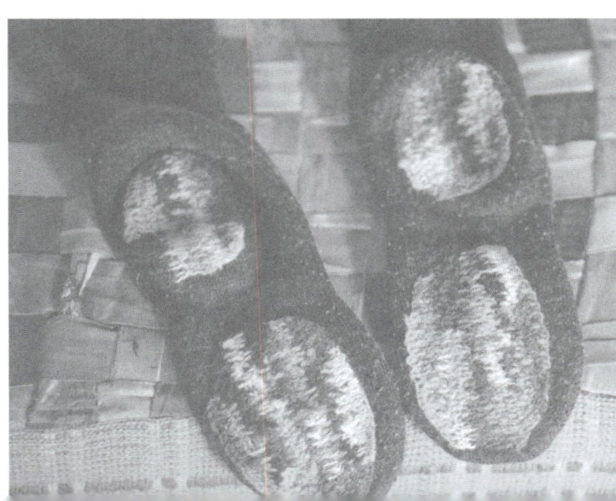

Use British wool that felts through washing

Hard pilling was removed with scissors to tidy up the surface. To get elasticity back in the soles, they were darned with wool yarn. Sheep's wool that has not been treated, will shrink a little every time you wash and turn partially into felt to fit the shape of your feet better. When you need to use a new thread, change colour to create the mosaic effect.

Applying zigzag parallel honeycomb from the WS leads to a beautiful zigzag pattern on the RS.

Zigzag parallel honeycomb as applied from the WS.

Slipper socks

Before

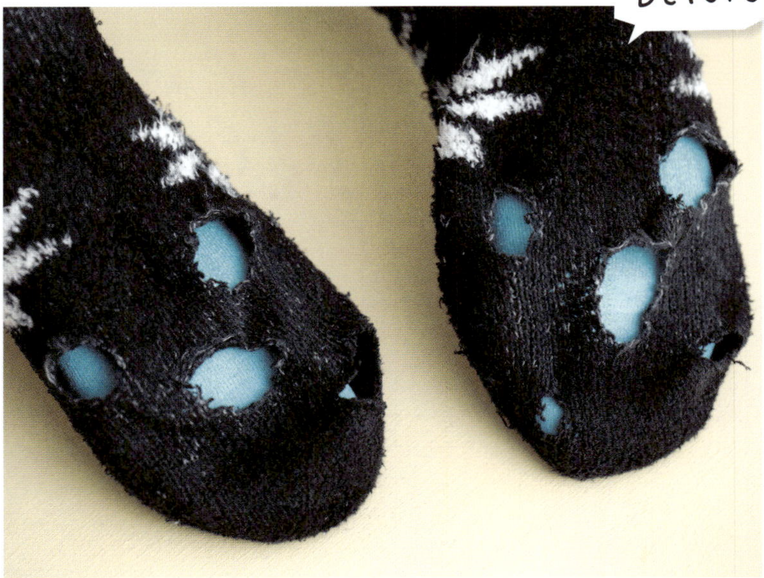

Case 30

The way socks become damaged varies from person to person. These synthetic fleece bed socks belong to an owner who often gets several coin-sized holes on the soles. The texture of the fleece is long gone, and the socks are covered in pilling.

Technique and threads used

Tights material patch applied (see page 16) and circular honeycomb (see page 20) worked from the RS and the WS using acrylic yarn.

Apply large circular honeycomb stitch.

The pilling of synthetic yarns can be hard in texture; it is important that you get rid of it carefully. The recommended material for the patch to fill the hole is from the briefs section of a pair of tights. Work round honeycomb in an area about 2cm (¾in) around the outside of the hole from both the RS and WS.

After

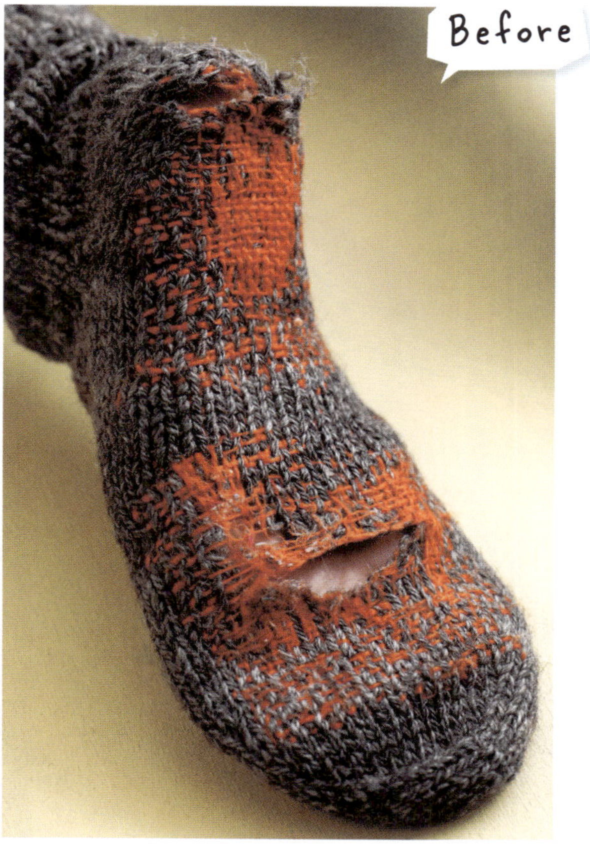

Case 31

This hand-knit house sock appeared in one of my previous books. Loving use had led to huge holes around the heel and the ball of the foot.

Technique and threads used

Tights material patch applied (see page 16) and English basket (see page 24) worked from the RS with sock yarn.

Using socks as patches

To achieve a strong finish, sock fabric was used to create the patches for the soles. The shape of the sole was copied using tracing paper and cut out to create a foot shaped template. Then the pattern was used to cut the patches, which were applied on the WS and then darned.

For the sole of the socks, the shin section of some old green socks was used for patches.

Handmade socks

Any darning technique can be used for hand-knit socks, but when the stitches are large, Swiss darning is recommended. Yarn that has thinned through friction can be fleshed out with extra thread for strength.

Before

Case 32

Gorgeous, colourful socks hand-knitted with space-dyed sock yarn. The ball of the foot has become thinned and the toe tips are worn out. Because the socks are made from a wool/synthetic blend yarn, the damage happened slowly, but steadily, unlike commercially bought socks.

Technique and threads used

Swiss darning (see page 29) using thread split from sock yarn.

The thickness and texture of wool is key

The key is to select wool that closely matches the thickness and texture of the original yarn used. By using the whole thickness of the yarn for heavily thinned areas, and threads split from the wool yarn (see page 11) for areas with minor damage you should achieve uniformity in thickness while ensuring elasticity in finish.

Swiss darning produces a beautiful finish even on the WS.

After

Case 33

These hand-knitted socks are made from a lovely multicoloured space-dyed yarn. Handmade socks are becoming more popular as they offer incomparable warmth. But the base of the heel and the ball area are worn out.

Technique and threads used

Heel: tights material patch applied (see page 16) and English basket stitch (see page 24) worked from the RS.

Ball: tights material patch applied and two-directional seed stitch (see page 22) worked with large stitches.

Threads used are made from a range of materials.

Enhancing the elasticity with two-directional seed stitch

For the sole of the heel, where elasticity is not necessary, apply the patch from the WS and work English basket stitch from the RS. To ensure comfort through elasticity for the ball area, apply the patch from the WS and work two-directional seed stitch from the WS.

The WS of the sock where the patch and two-directional seed stitch were applied.

Five-toe socks

Darning sticks, which are about the same thickness as the toe, can be used for darning toe socks. Once holes develop, it becomes harder to repair, so it is best to darn early when the damage is minor.

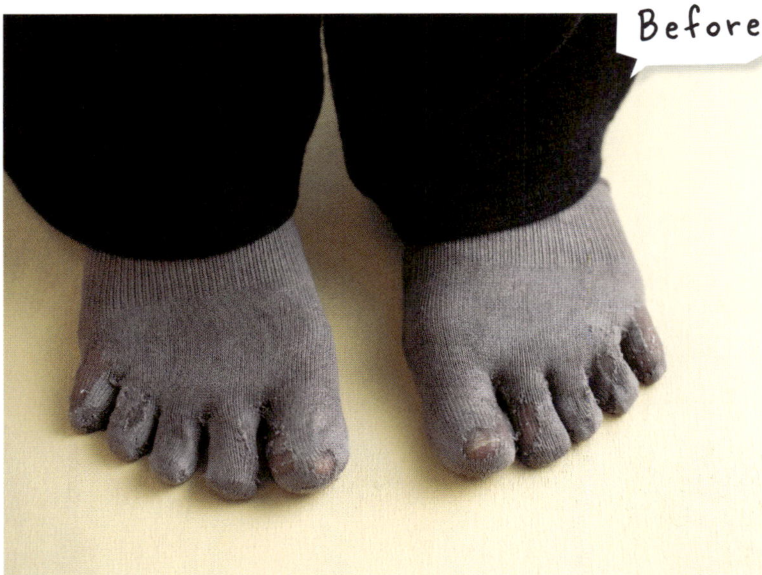

Before

Case 34

T's favourite silk socks, because T often gets cold toes. The whole toe area of the sock is damaged, some areas just slightly and some severely.

Technique and threads used

Parallel honeycomb stitch (see page 18) worked from the RS – wool/silk thread.

Using wool/silk thread that is gentle to the skin

Natural fibre yarn, made from a blend of extra-fine wool and silk was used. To ensure a flat, smooth finish, the repairs were stitched in parallel honeycomb, little by little, using a darning stick inside.

The WS is also finished flat to maintain comfort.

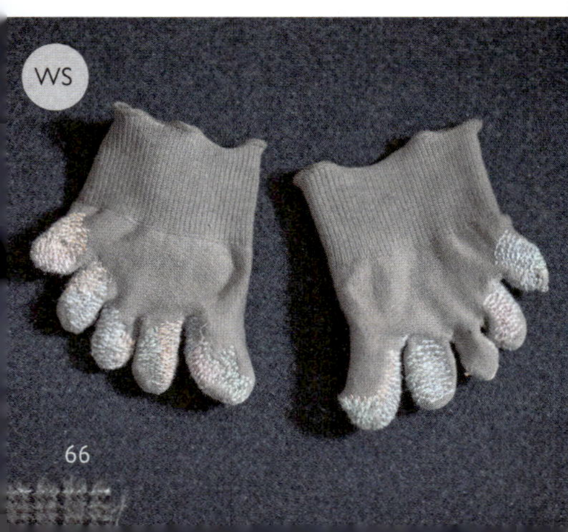

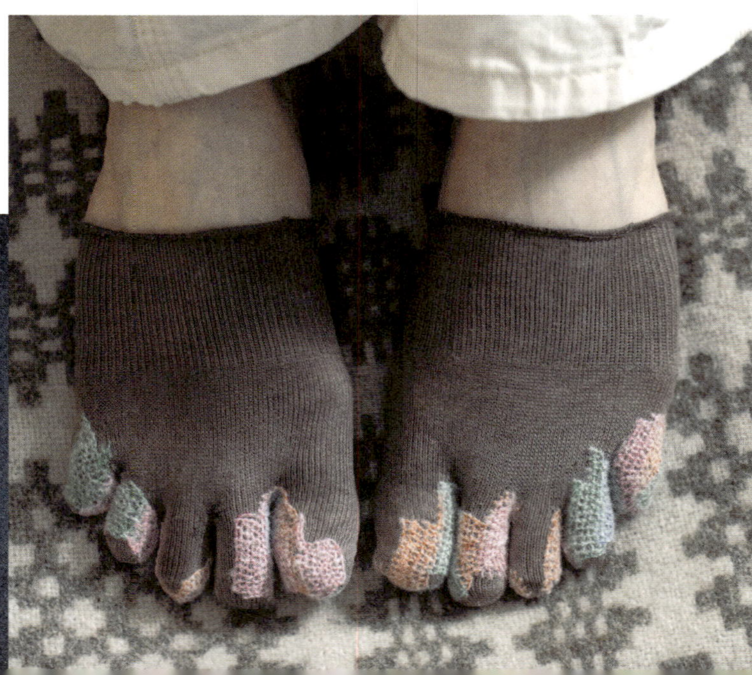

Case 35

For damage at the tip and base of toes, work round honeycomb stitch with a darning stick. For holes, apply a tights material patch from the WS.

Technique and threads used

a. Parallel honeycomb (see page 18) from the WS – acrylic yarn.

b. Circular honeycomb (see page 20) from the WS – acrylic yarn.

Case 36

For a hole at the tip of the toe, use a tights patch. Turn the sock WS out, insert the darning stick, apply the patch and secure with a rubber band. If you prefer to use natural fibres, a silk stocking/tights patch could be used.

Technique and threads used

Tights/stocking material patch applied and parallel honeycomb (see page 18) worked from WS – extra-fine acrylic yarn.

Part 10

Follow-up darning

Darned areas often become damaged again through repeated wear and wash. We call adding darning for such areas 'follow-up darning'. There is no need to take out the threads used before, and it is OK to use totally different threads when making additional repairs.

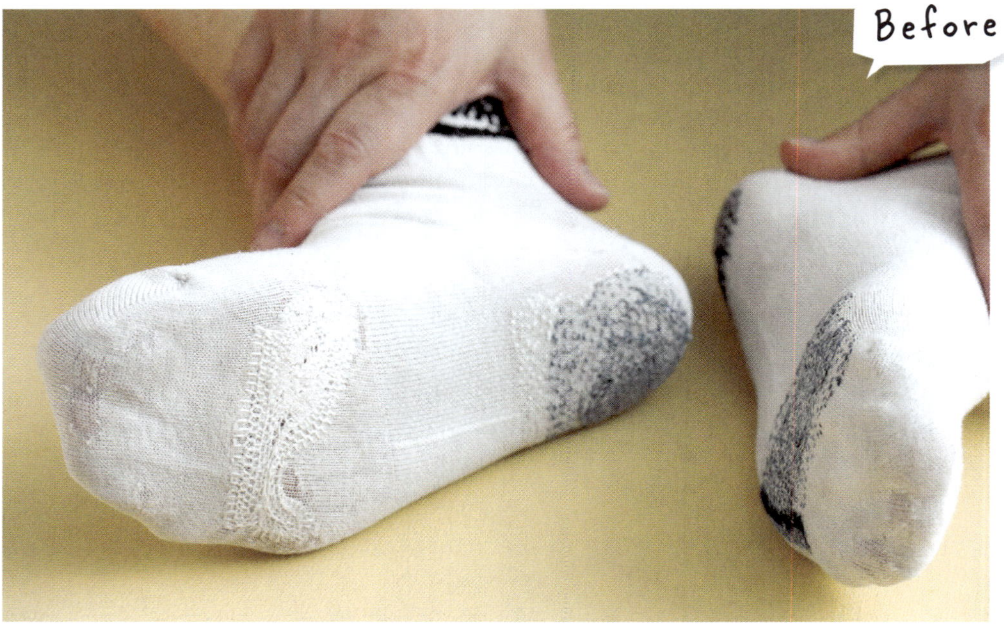

Case 37

Cotton sports socks loved by their university student owner. Every time a new heavily thinned area is found, various threads are used for darning, but in no time, there is another thinned area. Thinning in areas surrounding the previous darning areas is more obvious, rather than in the darned areas.

Thread used: silk/cotton thread

Tips for follow-up darning

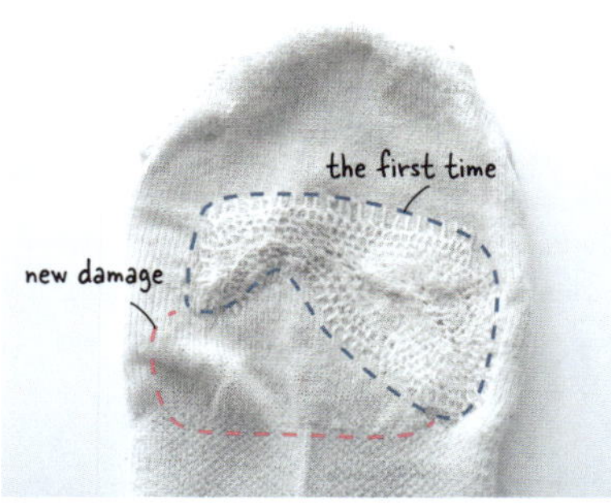

1 A thinned area has appeared below and to the left of the darned area, where round honeycomb was applied previously (white Sashiko thread).

2 Place the damaged area on the darning mushroom and secure firmly with a rubber band. To capture an area larger than the damage, use chalk to mark a frame around the area for darning. Make sure there is at a least 0.5–1cm (¼–⅜in) overlap with the old, darned area.

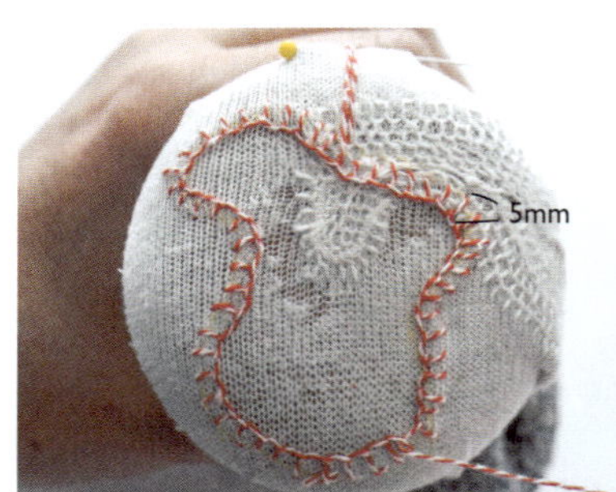

3 Work circular honeycomb stitch (see page 20) along the marked frame.

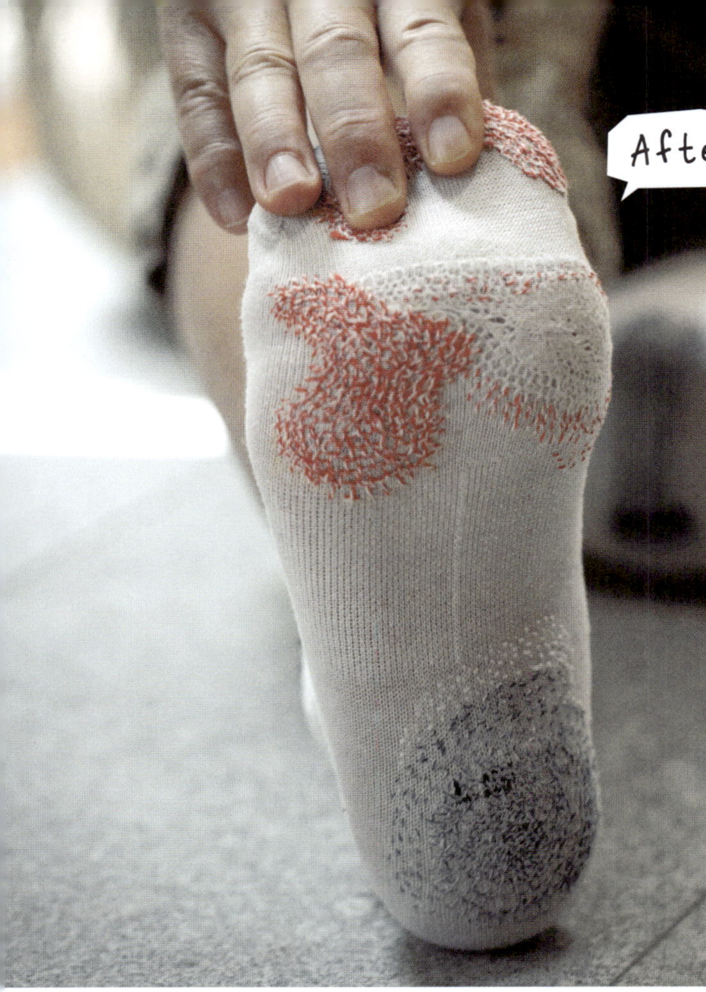

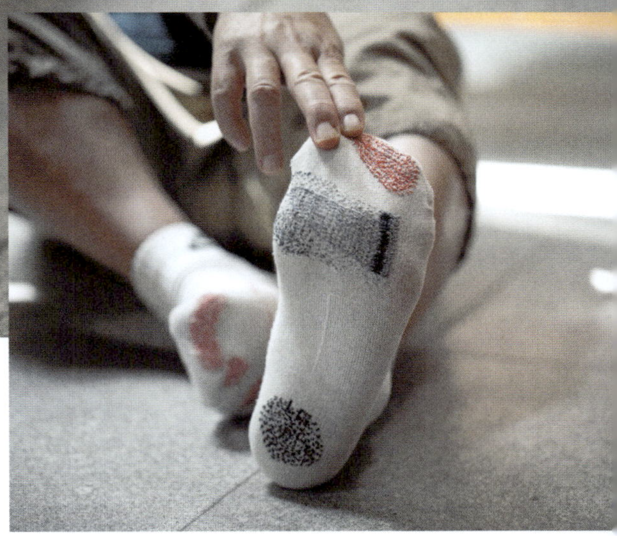

Once the damage progresses, simple seed stitches could help to extend life.

Observe the previous darning

The sock has been darned twice already. Before applying the third darning, it is a good idea to look closely at the threads and techniques used for repairs previously, to understand their success in terms of durability and comfort. Paying attention to how the darned area changes over time will help improve your repair skills.

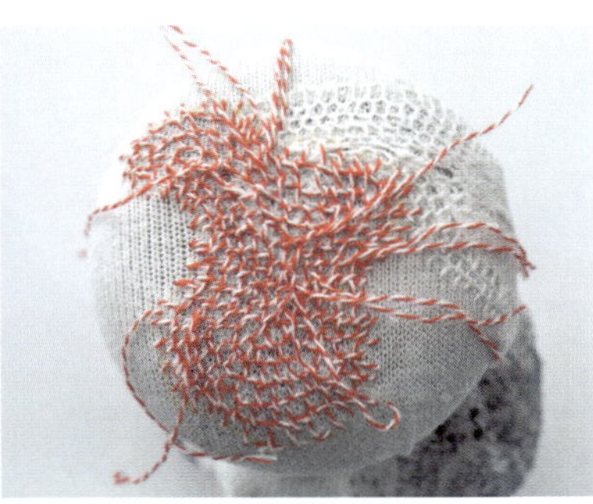

4 Stitch to fill the frame completely. Round honeycomb can be applied from either the RS or the WS.

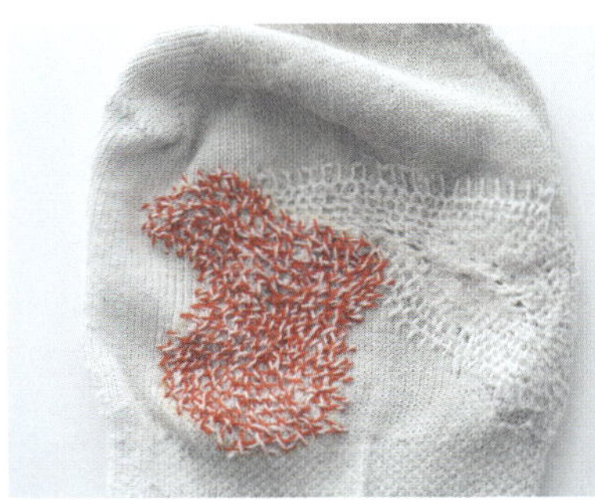

5 Both the starting and finishing ends are taken out on the WS to finish.

Ensure some overlap with the old darning

If you apply follow-up darning so that it overlaps with the previous darning, it helps reinforce properly. If you stitch over a wider area than the damaged section, it will survive longer. You can use any technique.

Follow-up darning

Case 38

The same style hand-knit room socks as shown in Case 31 but in a different colour. Again, large holes have appeared around the ball and the heel.

Technique and threads used

a. Swiss darning (see page 29) – extra-thick boucle mohair yarn.

b. Felted wool patch applied and seed stitch (see page 22) worked in the surrounding the area from the RS. Running stitches (see page 28) worked over the whole area, Sashiko square-shaped stitches added to bring the main body and the patch together – British wool yarn.

c. For reinforcement, seed stitch worked from the RS – British wool yarn.

The first time, basket darning was used.

Using knit material for patching

For the balls and the heel, a felted knit material patch was tacked on and seed and running stitches were used to repair. I'm looking forward to seeing how the darned areas become worn in two years' time.

Case 39

Cotton socks suitable for any season, repaired with circular honeycomb and seed stitches, but now a new area has become worn.

Technique and threads used

Circular honeycomb worked from both the WS and the RS (see page 20) and seed stitches (see page 22) – select thread freely from a range of raw material/yarn.

You can choose your favourite thread and technique

Every time a worn area is found, it is repaired diligently using a different colour thread and technique to keep the joy of wearing the socks. When the repeated follow-up darning ends up with socks that are not comfortable, perhaps that marks the end of the lifespan of the socks.

Part 11

Tights

The thinning at the crotch of these tights can be stitched using a kitchen bowl instead of a darning mushroom. Applying highly elastic honeycomb stitch will ensure they are comfortable to wear.

Case 40

Thick tights are a midwinter necessity. These had serious damage in the hip and the crotch: what to do?

Technique and threads used

Circular honeycomb stitch (see page 20) worked from the RS – green woolly thread, fluorescent yellow acrylic yarn.

Applying the briefs section of the tights

If it's minor thinning, you could apply circular honeycomb from the RS or the WS using a bowl. For heavily thinned areas, apply a tights patch, taken from the briefs section of the tights, add it from the WS and use a circular honeycomb stitch. You can repair leggings in a similar fashion.

Tip

Synthetic threads are recommended for their durability, particularly threads blended with wool.
Extra-fine wool (washable), cashmere or mohair yarn.

Attention: if you stitch too densely, it will be uncomfortable to wear.

Column 2

Socks to cherish, created by Antipast

In my darning work, I hear a lot of requests from fans of Antipast socks: 'my favourite Antipast socks are getting worn out. How do I darn them?' Antipast is a popular Japanese women's sock brand. I have often wondered – in this world where socks are usually seen as consumables – what makes these socks so special that people want to repair them and wear them for a longer period.

It is 33 years since Antipast was founded by Junko Jinushi and Kyoko Kato. When they started, women's socks were largely plain, and patterned socks were not meant for grown-ups in Japan. On the other hand, socks for men were available in simple colours, but made of excellent material, so the question of whether they could make women's socks with similarly high-quality materials but in brighter colours was what started Antipast.

Still, they faced a tough battle as yarns were only available in dull colours, and factories that accepted their ideas as 'fun' often encountered technical difficulties, so they had to explore design amid many constraints. It was a hard start, but the 90s saw a huge improvement in sock knitting machines and progress was made every day. Designs that were once deemed impossible, quickly became manufacturable. This led to the birth of beautiful Antipast socks, with delicate colour combinations and patterns that look like paintings fit for adults. Unprecedently beautiful, their socks became items that women matched shoes to and could even be the main item to dictate the day's fashion choices. Absolutely no compromise was made in their design or comfort. Today, they have dealings with boutiques not only in Japan but worldwide.

It is sad for wearers to see such socks – the results of such care and effort – become damaged and unwearable. Ms Kato and Ms Jinushi say, 'if you can apply darning and wear them even a little longer, that would be lovely.'

This was the origin of the collaboration between Antipast and Darning by HIKARU NOGUCHI, which started in 2022. I have been adding darning stitches to brand-new socks from Antipast, and Junko and Kyoko are enjoying the results, saying, 'It is exciting to see darning as it adds a new dimension and depth to the patterns.' In this collaboration, I stitch with attention to the balance between the pattern and colours of Antipast socks, but I am also hopeful they might give darning ideas to Antipast's customers for when their socks are damaged, allowing creative energy to arise from darning between the socks and wearers. Antipast socks provide a catalyst for such a chemical reaction to occur.

ANTIPAST

A brand that started with socks and was established by Junko Jinushi and Kyoko Kato who had previously worked as designers in printing, dying and weaving. Antipasto is Italian for hors d'oeuvre, which means, 'the main dish is you. Clothes and small items are hors d'oeuvre to make you shine and become even more beautiful.' With that as the key, underlying concept, they continue to create items with originality.

Extreme darning

The diverse and individualistic socks of darning lovers. They will not only last longer but also look much nicer!

From those undertaking their first ever darning challenge and the maniacs who are stuck deep in a darning quagmire – follow-up darning time and again – to those who darn decoratively, darners are a diverse bunch, as are their socks. As you can see here, there is no right answer to darning. Just do it! Use these examples for inspiration.

Colours selected to blend in
Darning on the toe tip looks like a manicure
Father's socks are evolving rapidly!
The soles look amazing!

Follow-up darning adds cushioning to the sole
Seed stitch layered on top of cable knit
Pricey, high-functionality socks - don't throw them away because of minor damage

One fun aspect of darning is the emergence of an almost 'parental' love that makes you nurture the socks, making you go through darning time and time again, commenting, 'right, this time you are damaged there, OK!'

These are the socks that are beloved by the owners, whose darning keeps them going just a bit longer, and a bit longer.

Darned socks shown by: Fumi Ito, Kumiko Inoko, Nami Kogushi, Junko Okuda, Yuko Kamakura, Kumiko Shimizu, Rie Takemoto, Maki Tobise.

Tell me, Ms Noguchi

Darning troubleshooting Q&A

Let's deal with all the questions you have, so that you can make a start!

Q1: Are there techniques simple enough for beginners?

A: All the techniques are simple enough for beginners. Parallel honeycomb, in particular, is highly recommended. For your first ever darning, try parallel honeycomb on a sock with a small, thinned area.

Q2: Are there materials suitable for reinforcing darning other than tights?

A: Old T-shirts, old inner layers – any thin material with some elasticity will do. Tights are recommended because their transparency allows you to see through the damaged area and it is easy to stitch through.

Q3: I can't stitch in a straight line

A: It is not necessary to stitch straight. Straight stiches are not necessarily right for darning. Wonky stitches are just as attractive. No need to fix them. Rather, enjoy the warped lines!

Q4: I can't darn as shown in the photos in the book

A: Each sock will have a different kind of damage. The shape of your foot, the way you walk, washing methods – these will all influence the wear and tear of your sock. So, it is not surprising that you cannot darn just like the examples in the photos. But that is exactly where the fun of darning lies; enjoy the darning experience by doing it your way.

Q5: I don't have worn socks or damaged clothes

A: Darning can make an excellent decoration. Give it a go, even if you don't have worn areas, you could try darning to decorate. Socks or clothes with your own darning decorations will become even more special.

Q6: I tried darning the damaged area, but now the area stands out and I am regretting it

A: Try a few small tambourine stitches (see page 28) or seed stitches (see page 22) around the area to create some 'darning buddies.' They make the darning less obvious and create a natural setting.

Q7: I am not confident about my sense of fashion, so I can cope with socks but hesitate to darn clothes

A: If you can darn stretchy material such as socks, then why not try other items? The key point is to use the thread with colours or texture that are attractive to you. Then they naturally turn into something you like.

Q8: I used tights on a hole and darned from the back. When I turned it over, I could see the tights material in between stitches and it feels strange

A: It will not affect its durability, so if you don't mind it, leave it as it is. If it bothers you, you could use thin thread from the front and apply honeycomb stitch to fill the material. Beware that this could make the area stiff if the stitches are too close together or overlap.

Q8: When I use tights materials for the holes and darn, sometimes it runs or tears

A: You can continue darning ignoring the runs. When it tears, put a new piece of tights on top and keep stitching. Once you finish stitching, fasten off the thread, and cut the tights material at the edges.

Epilogue

When you hear the term 'darning' you think about socks – the most common damage you will come across every day occurs on socks. Back in the 1970s, when I was small, I remember my grandmother using a light bulb to darn socks. Today, socks with great design and durability are available at three pairs for 1000 yen; socks have become consumables. But sometimes you can become attached to socks and value them because they are comfortable, even if they were cheap.

For the Japanese, who take off shoes when entering a house, socks and their damage is something that we pay attention to every day. Some of you may feel attached to your socks and want to start darning but have concerns and negative thoughts about your ability.

There is absolutely no need to worry that you cannot darn 'as beautifully as the examples in this book.' Indeed, there is no such thing as doing well or badly, or right or wrong in darning. The design of the sock, the material, your foot shape, your walking style, laundry methods, feel to the skin – all will be different. I just want you to give darning a go simply because 'it looks fun' using this book as a guide to repair damaged or even non-damaged socks.

Introduced in this book are the easiest darning methods, which can lead to the best finish with a good feel and durability, discovered through my research, development and through teaching darning to 1,500 people every year. The stitches that point this way and that are not 'untidy' but evidence of dancing stitches generated through fun. Good if you become a darning maniac and stitch madly. Great, if you just give it a go once and give up after one sock and throw it away after darning. The sense in your hands and experience of having made an extra effort with a needle and thread will definitely spice up your everyday life.

To inspire more interest and understanding, I hope to continue to introduce various techniques through video clips on Instagram: @hikaru_noguchi_design

I would like to give my thanks to the people who lent us their damaged socks, those extreme darners who lent us their darned socks, members of the darning team for *Darning by Hikaru Noguchi*, and the editorial team.

HIKARU NOGUCHI

Hikaru is a textile designer who has participated in shows and exhibitions all over the world, and her work is sold in boutiques and department stores in London, Paris, New York and Tokyo. Hikaru moved to England from Japan in 1989 to study constructed textiles and after completing her studies at Middlesex University she developed new and innovative textiles with designers including Tom Dixon, Topshop and projects for Barneys, Browns, Paul Smith, Takashimaya New York and many others. Other publications include *Beyond Darning: Creative mending techniques*, *Darning: Repair, make, mend*, *Creative Mending* and *Made in France: Knitting*. Works globally, pushing boundaries through textile design, consulting, and writing. Hikaru spearheaded the recent resurgence of mending and conducts many workshops in Japan and abroad including via zoom. She designs original tools as well as threads.

Homepage: www.hikarunoguchi.com

Information about workshops and original products: https://hikarunoguchi.shop

Instagram: @hikaru_noguchi_design @darning_by_hikaru_noguchi

DARNING SOCKS

Published by Quickthorn Ltd
Lower Street Atelier, 19a Lower Street, Stroud, Gloucestershire, GL5 2HT UK
info@quickthornbooks.com
www.quickthornbooks.com

Publisher: Katy Bevan
Printed in the UK by Cambrian
Printed on uncoated FSC certified paper
British Library Cataloguing in Publication Data applied for
ISBN 978-1-0683215-2-8

Originally published as HAJIMETE NO KUTSUSHITA DARNING (NV70776)

Photographer: Akemi Kurosaka